A nostalgic look at

BIRMINGHAM TRAMS

1933-1953

Volume I
The northern routes

197

David Harvey

Silver Link Publishing Ltd

This book is dedicated to my grandfather, Harry Harvey, who died in the same year that the Birmingham trams were abandoned. He took me, at a very tender age, to see trams at the Perry Barr terminus and started an enthusiasm that has remained with me ever since.

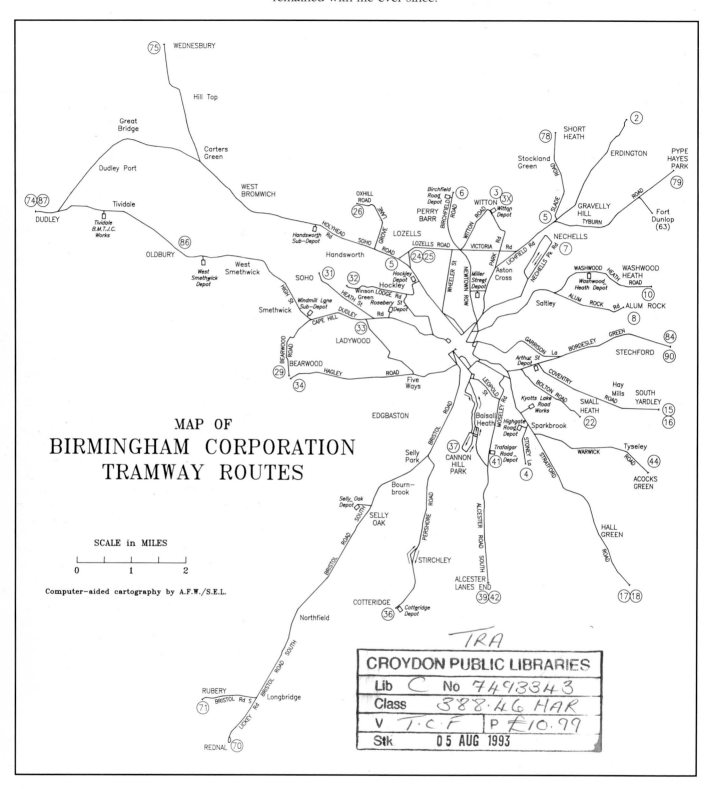

MAP OF
BIRMINGHAM CORPORATION
TRAMWAY ROUTES

SCALE in MILES

0   1   2

Computer–aided cartography by A.F.W./S.E.L.

Map of Birmingham Corporation tramway routes

This map shows the whole of the tramway network, including the northern routes featured in this book, but does not purport to show the system at any given date, being intended principally to locate each route to scale. Only the route numbers of regular all-day tramcar services are shown.

For detail of trackwork and locations of short working turning points, see the definitive map by J. C. Gillham, extracts of which are given in each chapter.

CONTENTS

ACKNOWLEDGEMENTS

THIS book would not have been possible but for the work of all the photographers who are credited within the main text.

Special thanks must be given to Geoffrey Morant, whose efforts in tracking down the extremely rare colour photographs of the Birmingham system was invaluable. W. J. Wyse's helpfulness in allowing his colour slides to be reproduced was instrumental in starting to gather together the collection of colour photographs that would eventually form the basis of those included in this and the second volume. Equally invaluable was Keith Terry's expertise in identifying colour slides of the system from the Leeds Transport Historical Society's collection.

I am most grateful to W. A. Camwell, John Edgington, F. Lloyd Jones, L. W. Perkins, C. C. Thornburn and Ray Wilson for allowing so much of their respective photographic collections of the Birmingham municipal system to be used. I am indebted to John Stanford of the Birmingham Transport Historical Group for all his comments, especially those regarding the dating of individual photographs, and to Richard Weaver for his valuable editing contribution.

I am also most grateful to Tom Rowley, who provided me with background information, especially regarding historical data about the licensing trade, and to Roger de Boer whose knowledge of the local battery-electric dairy and dustcart fleets proved to be most useful.

Two people, however, deserve a special mention. Peter Jaques spent a great deal of time checking factual data and amplified this with a considerable amount of information from his own extensive records. Interestingly, he even discovered a photograph of himself standing next to a tramcar!

A number of years ago I discovered the quite splendid photographs of Norman Glover. His pictures appear throughout this volume and his contributions in the form of personal reminiscences and his editing of the text have been extremely helpful.

My thanks also go to Stan Letts and Arthur Whitehouse for producing the general layout map of the Birmingham tram system, and to John Gillham for allowing me to use extracts from his most detailed Birmingham track layout maps.

Finally, as always, thanks to my wife, Diana, without whose hard work in typing the draft manuscript, critical comments, encouragement, patience and letting me off washing up duties, this book would have been impossible.

© David Harvey 1993

Route maps © J. C. Gillham 1982
General system map © Stan Letts and Arthur Whitehouse

First published in June 1993

British Library Cataloguing in Publication Data

A catalogue record for this book is available from the British Library

ISBN 1 85794 014 8

Silver Link Publishing Ltd
Unit 5
Home Farm Close
Church Street
Wadenhoe
Peterborough PE8 5TE
Tel/fax (08015) 4-4-0

Printed and bound in Great Britain

FOREWORD

Norman Painting OBE MA

(known to millions as Phil Archer in BBC Radio 4's The Archers) remembers his student days in Birmingham in the 1940s

BIRMINGHAM trams were a basic and indispensable part of my university life. Twice a day, sometimes four times, and on occasion six, I would rattle on my carefree way from one half of the University to the other. I was in the Arts Faculty, which, with the Law Faculty and the Department of Education, was housed in Mason College, Edmund Street (where the City Library now stands). The rest of the University, the greater part of it, was at Edgbaston, and I remember the Vice-Chancellor, Sir Raymond Priestley (who went with Scott to the Pole) saying that the University was in two parts that did not form a whole.

He was right - it was like the Earth and the Moon linked together. And that link was the tram.

At least once a day I would run down Hill Street to catch the tram at Navigation Street, and leap off some ten or so bone-shaking minutes later at the bottom of Edgbaston Park Road, running up to the Union Building, the Barber Institute or the Senior Training Corps Headquarters, only to repeat the whole process later. I should perhaps say 'we', because there was usually a group of us - students tend to hunt in packs. When I realise that today, some 50 years later, I have become a

happy loner, and the idea of running anywhere, least of all uphill, has an odd feel to it, those days of unbounded animal energy seem like part of another world - just like the long-vanished trams on which so many student hours were passed.

They were scarcely comfortable, those trams. I remember those rows of wooden slatted seats, with backrests that could be reversed according to the direction of travel. On the upper deck an additional semi-circle of seats fitted into the rounded ends of the coachwork. These were favoured by students as we could continue our group discussions more conveniently than if sitting in rows.

Today, when I leave the BBC studios and walk up Pebble Mill Road to the Bristol Road hotel where I usually stay, the ghosts of those tram-travelling days are very near. There the tree-lined central reservation still remains, forming a natural dual-carriageway, with the old tram-track in the middle, and many memories of lost days are rekindled. But memories sometimes bring unanswered questions. Why, for example, was there that meshed cow-catcher at the front of a vehicle that was going nowhere more rural than The Lickeys? Why on straight speedy sections did the tall trams sway in such a confident, cradling way, and roll in a menacing sea-sick-producing manner like a sailing vessel on water? And apart from the cheery tuneful 'ding-dong' of the conductor's bell, why did the tram produce such a friendly, almost melodious sound as the speed increased? Is memory up to its rose-tinted tricks again? Were they really so user-friendly? None of us who used them ever complained.

Not that my use of the tram was exclusively confined to that stretch from the city to Edgbaston. There were occasions when we went to the southernmost end of the line, ready for walks on the Lickey Hills, or army training and route marches. One of the simple joys of the terminus was to watch the conductor (or was it the driver?) showing precise skill (or the opposite) as he manoeuvred the end of the trolley pole from one end of the roof of the tram to the other to reverse the direction. Sometimes he'd engage the overhead cable in one, and earn a small cheer. Sometimes not. It always seemed that if he didn't do it first time, it could take any number of attempts before contact was made, especially in rainy or windy weather, and often to the sound of a muffled cheer or ironic applause. What I remember is a single arm with a pair of narrow connectors like bobbins or large cotton-reels at the end, and forked so that it gripped the cable. Getting that cable into such a narrow space could not have been easy.

Photo: Stuart Martin

In those athletic days when stairs were no hazard, we students nearly always shot upstairs to the upper deck (I don't recall doing anything slowly). We didn't go upstairs to smoke necessarily - smoking wasn't allowed on the lower deck - but because, other things apart, most of us couldn't afford it. But we did favour the upper deck, and my memories of the 70, 71 and 72 trams in the years 1942-46 seem always to be of looking down - down on the traffic, down on the people on the pavements, and, most vividly of all, looking down on not very memorable front gardens, as Horsefair became Bristol Road, and shops became Edgbaston houses, some of them Georgian and most of them looking very seedy under wartime decorating restrictions.

Birmingham trams were, of course, usually serviced by Birmingham people. The conductor was often a man of scathing Brummie wit, half envious, half suspicious of undergraduates. Some of them were cheerful enough, but it would be sentimental and untrue to say that the Birmingham tram conductor was always warm and friendly. He - and it usually was a he! - was quite wrong if he thought we were part of a privileged few, yet he could not help treating us as if we were overgrown schoolchildren. Even our frequent appearance in STC khaki uniform didn't seem to modify his unspoken view that we ought to be away at the war. (STC, incidentally, meant Senior Training Corps and not, as we sometimes convinced polite enquirers, Shock Troop Corps.)

That pained indulgence with which the tram conductor treated us was well illustrated when one sunny evening I was returning from Edgbaston to the city. I was sitting at the front of the tram upstairs on the semi-circular seats. My companions, deep in animated talk as usual, handed the conductor the correct fare almost as if performing some reflex action, without breaking the conversation. (There were no student passes or season tickets then.) My turn to pay came. I suddenly realised that, unlike my fellow students, I hadn't the exact fare (which if I remember right was threepence). With an apology I handed the conductor all I had - a pound note.

He gave me a very long-suffering Brummie look. With a heavy sigh he said, 'Well, you'll have to have all small'. The meaning of this dark remark was soon made clear when he counted out the change to me in threepenny bits, seventy-nine of them. They were the thick, heavy, straight-sided brass-coloured ones, not the little silvery threepenny Joeys which they'd replaced. They seemed to weigh a ton. I walked like a deep-sea diver, heavily weighted before submerging, though I had more than a suspicion that the conductor had far less weighty change in his wallet. But

these youngsters needed taking down a peg sometimes.

There was one day, though, when undergraduates in academic gowns were welcomed, or at least tolerated, on all the city's transport vehicles. This was Hospital Rag Day when we could board any tram or bus and rattle our collecting tins at the passengers. On this one day it was possible to wander over the whole city, and I must have travelled over it all, north and south, exhorting the populace to 'Help the Hospital!', breaking all the rules by boarding a tram or leaping off it while it was in motion.

I have never pretended that Birmingham was my first choice of university, for from a very early age I had always wanted to go to Oxford. I did, after four years, eventually get there. It seems as if I have always been hopelessly in love with the place, and I grow more besotted every day. So it can easily be imagined that my undergraduate days in Birmingham were very different from my dreams of life in an ancient university.

Instead of quiet quads enclosed by ancient buildings of honey-coloured stone, there was the Victorian Gothic of Mason College in an island of noisy traffic. Instead of placid and static life in college, there was commuting by tram from city to Edgbaston, from lecture-hall and refectory to the Union for play rehearsals and student government meetings. Instead of the mellow atmosphere which only centuries of tranquillity can create, there was the noise and bustle and energy of the young and thrusting Second City. Instead of the High, there was the Bristol Road. Instead of the river and leisurely punting, there was a little row-boat on a small local reservoir. All very different; and yet those days in Birmingham were golden days, heroic days in spite of insufficient money and wartime deprivations. What might have seemed a disappointment, a second best, turned out to be anything but that; those years were magical, stimulating, unforgettable, even if they were only the prelude to a dream fulfilled.

They were frenetic, restless, challenging and creative times, and though occasionally life was tough and uncomfortable, I find I look back with almost undiluted pleasure at one of the most exciting and fulfilling four years of my life.

Running like a continuous thread through the whole period were those dear old indispensable trams, without which a student life in those days of little or no private transport would have been impossible. And looking back, no one could be more surprised that I was when I found that of all the facets of my student life in Birmingham, what I remembered with the greatest affection, and, curiously, with considerable gratitude, were those rattling old bone-shakers, Birmingham's long-lost trams.

INTRODUCTION

THIS year sees the 40th anniversary of the final closure of the Birmingham Corporation tramway system. The Birmingham tramway fleet was well known for its high standard of mechanical maintenance and its immaculate dark blue and primrose paintwork. Unfortunately, to most people every Birmingham tram looked virtually the same. These tall, gaunt, even stately trams were part of the street scene in the city for 49 years, and perhaps it was only when they had gone that the public realised that part of their own lives had also disappeared.

The main problem with any history of Birmingham's municipal transport is the size of the operation - it was deceptively big. The city has a population that is still around the million mark and as a result the transport infrastructure has always had to be equally large. Birmingham had a total of 843 trams, a maximum number of 825 in service, 20 depots and yards, some 45 main routes and a total of 80.5 route miles. It was the largest 3 ft 6 in gauge system in the United Kingdom and was only exceeded in size by the tramways in London, Glasgow and Manchester.

This book continues the 'Nostalgic look at' theme by placing the Birmingham tram in its social and historical context. Just as trams have been consigned to history, so have many of the streets and roads through which they ran. The photographs, nearly all of which have never been published before, capture moments in a period of time from about 1933 until 1953, and will bring back memories to those interested not just in Birmingham trams but also the street scenes and the many long-demolished buildings.

All cities are dynamic, in that they are constantly evolving, but the passing of the tramcar in Birmingham on 4 July 1953 corresponded with the start of one of the largest urban renewal programmes in post-war Britain. Put in simple terms, the trams' disappearance from the city was one of the first markers of dramatic change in Birmingham, which would eventually result in the partial pedestrianisation of the city centre, the extension of the central area along Broad Street to encompass the enormous investment of the International Conference Centre, the development of the 'Heartlands' project in Aston, Saltley and Bordesley, and the removal of vast tracts of old Victorian inner city housing. Perhaps, most con-

tentiously, many of the small workshops and factories which enabled Birmingham to be known throughout the world as 'The City of a Thousand and One Trades' were also demolished. These areas were the domain of the tram, as were the inter-war suburbs that developed along many of the main arterial routes out of the city. Birmingham was at the forefront of the development of reserved track along the routes of suburbia, and throughout the 1920s new route extensions to serve the ever-enlarging suburban area were built.

As early as 1923 the standard outline of the totally enclosed Birmingham tramcar had evolved. The constant programme of rebuilding and remotoring was somewhat masked by the conservatively styled, rocker-panelled, hexagonal-dashed, wooden-framed, $16\frac{1}{2}$-ton conveyances which could sway along the Bristol Road South reserved track at speeds which left behind any competing bus.

By then, however, the future of the trams was already becoming more doubtful. Although two experimental lightweight trams were delivered in 1929 and 1930, three unremunerative routes had already been closed. Within two years the argument about the next generation of vehicle type, between the trolleybus and the oil-engined bus, had already gone against 'the silent service', and the development of the tramcar in Birmingham became superfluous.

This book looks at the Birmingham tramway routes that remained mainly on the northern and south-eastern sides of the city from about 1933, 20 years before the final abandonment. It examines each group of routes by undertaking a pictorial survey of trams in their street setting from the city to the outer terminus.

The routes covered are firstly those which fit loosely into the geographical pattern and were abandoned earliest. This includes the Coventry Road services, which were the only ones to be replaced by trolleybuses after 1933, and the Stratford Road and Warwick Road routes. The routes to Lodge Road, Ladywood, Washwood Heath and Alum Rock, Perry Barr, Witton and Lozells as well as the last group of services to be withdrawn, those to Short Heath, Pype Hayes and Erdington, are also covered in this volume. It is intended that the second volume will look at the southerly and westerly services.

A BRIEF HISTORY OF BIRMINGHAM CORPORATION TRAMWAYS (1873-1929)

THE first horse trams in Birmingham ran on 11 September 1873 from Colmore Row to Hockley Brook as an extension of the standard gauge (4 ft 8$\frac{1}{2}$ in) route from Dudley Port to Hockley Brook. The route was the first tangible result of a number of proposals that had started as far back as August 1860 with the pioneer of the horse tram, none other than George Francis Train. A second route was opened on 17 June 1876 from Suffolk Street to the Malt Shovel in Bournbrook via Bristol Road. These pioneering routes were the only standard gauge tram routes ever to be built in Birmingham.

The horse tramway in Birmingham never really developed as it did, for example, in London or Newcastle, because other forms of traction had become available. In fact, the West Midlands area was one of the pioneer regions for mechanical tram operation in the country. John Downes of Birmingham had designed a steam tramway locomotive which had been constructed in 1875 by Henry Hughes of the Falcon Works in Loughborough, and it worked experimentally at various times in January 1876 between Birmingham Snow Hill and West Bromwich and in the Hill Top area near Wednesbury.

The first regular steam service, by the Birmingham and Aston Tramways Co, began operation from Old Square to Witton on Boxing Day 1882. Within Birmingham, the Birmingham Central Company (later City of Birmingham Tramways) opened routes to Perry Barr on 25 November 1884 and along Moseley Road on 29 December 1884, and these were quickly followed by further double-deck steam tram operations along Stratford Road (11 May 1885) and Coventry Road (16 January 1886).

The Birmingham and Midland Tramways Company opened a line from Lionel Street, near Birmingham city centre, along Dudley Road to the city boundary on 6 July 1885, and this was soon extended to Oldbury, West Bromwich and Dudley.

Unlike the horse tram routes, which had all been to standard gauge, the steam tram system was built to the 3 ft 6 in gauge. This was universal across Birmingham and the Black Country and allowed for through running into West Bromwich, Smethwick and Dudley. A new BCT horse tram route to Nechells, opened in March 1885, was also built to the narrow gauge.

On 24 March 1888 BCT opened its cable tramway from Colmore Row to the New Inns in Handsworth via Hockley. This replaced the standard gauge horse tramway, while the Bournbrook route along Bristol Road to Dawlish Road was similarly converted from animal power on 24 July 1890. The method of traction employed here was, unusually, electric accumulator cars. Twelve cars were built, looking very similar to the BCT cable cars, but they had lead acid batteries. These tended to be

unreliable because of battery failure, but the route continued until 14 May 1901.

Steam traction continued to develop, with covered-topped trailers and coke refuelling yards at the termini. Despite extensions, on Stratford Road as late as 1899, the advent of electric traction elsewhere meant that steam days were numbered.

Meanwhile, in nearby Walsall, on 1 January 1893, the South Staffordshire Company opened electrified tram routes to Wednesbury, Darlaston and Bloxwich with 16 small four-wheeled tramcars. This was the second overhead trolley system to be opened in the country, after Leeds. The development of electric traction in Birmingham was, however, to take place some eight years later.

Birmingham Corporation had constructed all the tramways itself, but had leased the track to the various companies. In 1900 the City of Birmingham Tramways Company (CBT) offered to replace the unsatisfactory accumulator cars with overhead electric trams on Bristol Road, but without altering any existing leasing agreements on the route. This effectively meant that a trial could be conducted using the overhead system for 11 years. The CBT line opened on 14 May 1901 with 15 cars built by the Electric Railway & Tramway Carriage Works Ltd (ER&TCW), later the United Electric Car Co Ltd (UEC), running from Suffolk Street to Chapel Lane, Selly Oak, half a mile further on from the old battery car terminus.

From then on CBT continued to convert steam tram lines to electric traction. On 19 September 1904, in Aston Manor UDC, the company converted the former steam tram line to electric operation from Aston Church and Aston Cross to Steelhouse Lane. It used the track from the same city terminus to, initially, Aston Brook Street, which had been opened on 4 January 1904 by the Corporation using the large 1-20 Class bogie cars.

CBT opened a new route from Victoria Road to Six Ways, Aston, on 27 October 1904, and in December of that year the service was extended to Aston Station. A further extension by CBT to Gravelly Hill had to be operated by single-deck cars, including some converted cable car 'toast-racks', until the low bridge at the station was replaced on 25 March 1906.

The Coventry Road route was opened by CBT on 29 March 1904 between Yardley and Small Heath, with through running into Station Street in the city centre from 23 February 1905. The Pershore Road branch along Pershore Road opened on 20 May 1904, being extended from the Breedon Cross, Stirchley, to Cotteridge one month later on 23 June. The company's Lodge Road route opened on 14 April 1906 and to Ladywood on 17 October, while in the east of the city, the route to

Bordesley Green via Fazeley Street opened on 24 November 1906.

The big year for electric municipal expansion in the city was 1907, after all the CBT steam tram service leases expired, other than the Handsworth cable route and the Bristol Road routes operated from Cotteridge and Bournbrook depots. The final horse trams ran to Nechells on the last day of September 1906 and the last steam trams worked along Stratford Road and Moseley Road on New Year's Eve 1906.

On the following morning trams from the 21-70 Class and most of the 71-220 Class were operating the new Birmingham Corporation Tramways' services to Sparkhill, Stoney Lane, Leopold Street, Cannon Hill, Kings Heath, Bolton Row, Alum Rock, Nechells and Newtown Row. The electric tram had now really taken over the city's transport system, and with the 71-220 Class came 8 ft 6 in radial trucks and the first top covers delivered new with the trams. The Board of Trade, however, still insisted on open balconies on four-wheel-trucked cars on the 3 ft 6 in gauge, so the earlier 21 and 221 Class Brill cars, with their short 6-foot wheelbase trucks, were top covered retrospectively, the last one not being completed until midway through the 1920s.

Extensions to Alcester Lanes End, Kings Heath, took place on 29 January 1907, while Erdington was reached with due ceremony on 22 April. Ten days later the Washwood Heath route was opened. For the next few years the system, after this rapid expansion, remained fairly static.

The service to Perry Barr was fraught with problems connected with through running in Aston (see page 60), a situation that lasted until 1909. Various cross-city lines in the High Street, Moor Street and Digbeth areas allowed for links to be made between Sparkbrook to Saltley and Small Heath to Nechells.

The remaining CBT leases were due to expire on 30 June 1911, and sixty low-height top-covered cars were ordered from United Electric Car Co (UEC) in November 1910, giving complete route availability within the city. They were numbered 301-360 and in June 1911 an extra forty cars to a similar design (they were 6 inches longer to accommodate the hand-brake) were ordered to supplement the cars in poor condition that had been taken over from CBT.

CBT operation came to an end after 31 December 1911 when the Corporation took over the assets and the tracks on the Bristol, Coventry and Stratford Roads, acquiring as part of the settlement the depots at Bournbrook and Yardley. In addition, sixty-one trams were taken over; 451-452 were two of the three CBT 178-180 Class of bogie cars, while 453-472/481-501 were either CBT or Brush-built four-wheelers and 473-480 were the ex-Small Heath bogie cars converted to four-wheelers in 1904 after about one year of use.

The result of these takeovers was that most of the main arterial routes out of the city were now equipped with electric tramways. The most noticeable exceptions were along Hagley Road and to Harborne, where local residents, backed by the Calthorpe family and the local MP, Neville Chamberlain, took grave exception to the intrusion of the overhead trolley wires.

In the two years between the final takeover of the CBT and the outbreak of the First World War there were several significant developments. In November 1911 an order for fifty cars was placed with UEC; intended to be identical to the 361 Class, these were the trams of the 401 Class, which spent virtually the whole of their working lives working from Moseley Road depot. They were fitted with the Spencer and Dawson air and oil brake which was designed by the aforesaid gentlemen in Bradford for use on steep hills. The brake had been adopted to cater for the steep 1 in 13 gradient of Leopold Street and was designed to fail in the 'on' position.

Further extensions took place in the years leading up to the First World War; the main one was, at long last, the route along Hagley Road, which opened on 11 June 1913 and which was, for about three months in 1914, the location for an experimental first class service using the newest bogie cars. The trams concerned belonged to the 512-586 Class, which had been built by UEC on Mountain & Gibson Burnley maximum traction bogies. They were virtually eight-wheel equivalents of the 301 Class with their enclosed platforms and open balconies, and became the forerunners of nearly all the trams built for Birmingham. The 512 Class trams were also used on the Handsworth services, which had recently converted from cable operation, and the Moseley Road group of routes.

The gap in the fleet numbers was taken up by the 61 trams that had been taken over by CBT; these were all open-toppers running in the CBT livery of either green and cream or lake and cream, and were used widely on either peak-hour duties or football specials. The two bogie cars, 451 and 452, were cut down to single-deck condition in 1917, along with one of the small ex-Bristol Road four-wheelers, 509, for trailer experiments on the Nechells route. These were not altogether successful and the two ex-CBT cars were eventually re-converted to double-decker status with the two large ex-CBT bogie cars being top-covered for the first time.

The only route opened during the Great War, on 2 February 1916, was along Warwick Road as far as Broad Road, Acocks Green, but short of its intended destination because of legal problems over widening the road.

At the end of the war, the main problems was lack of track and vehicle maintenance. Fifty bogie trams were ordered from Brush of Loughborough and entered service from March 1920 as 587-636; these were the last tramcars built for Birmingham with open balconies, and marked the start of a period of considerable expansion, both in terms of the route developments and the number of tramcars. After this order no fewer than 207 new bogie trams were to be delivered, of which all but two were to the same standard outline.

The first new route opened after the war was the second to be built on reserved track in the city, and was laid out on a reservation along the newly constructed road to the Dunlop Rubber Factory. This was opened on 13 May 1920 and was to be the first of many reserved tracks to be built in Birmingham. The problems over the road widths in Acocks Green were finally ended in 1922, and the Warwick Road route was extended into the village on 9 October. However, it was the developments on the southwest side of the city which were the most spectacular.

On the 26 November 1922 the Nechells tram route was abandoned. It had always been lightly trafficked and had only required twelve trams from Washwood Heath to run it. The route was basically a single line with passing loops, and the track had become badly worn. The decision was made not to renew it, and to adopt a new mode of propulsion. The result was the introduction of a fleet of twelve Railless top-covered double-deck trackless vehicles. The significance of this event was that it was the first time in this country that a tram route had been replaced by trolleybuses.

Expansion, however, was still the Corporation's policy. The tram services along Bristol Road were gradually extended to Northfield (1 October 1923), to Longbridge (17 December 1923) and to Rednal (14 April 1924), with a branch from Longbridge to Rubery opening on 8 February 1926. These were, with the exception of the Selly Oak and Northfield shopping centres, all on reserved sleeper track and this enabled high-speed running to take place as part of the normal schedules.

Further street track was opened when the Alum Rock route was extended to the Pelham public house on 14 October 1925, while the Bordesley Green route was extended along a central reservation on 4 November.

The interwar building of houses on open land was quite phenomenal. In the ten years following 1919 some 30,000 municipal houses were constructed, and this initially led to the extension of tram routes on the main arterial routes. The lower densities of the housing estates being built was in line with the Housing, Town Planning Act of 1909; this developed the ideas of Ebenezer Howard, who had first outlined the garden city idea, and effectively ended the building of dark-alleyed terraced housing, so typical of many inner parts of British cities. As far as the Birmingham trams were concerned, although these reserved tracks were seen as an integral development of the suburbs, it was soon discovered that buses going into the estates would be a more flexible option for public transport. Therefore the seeds of the demise of the tramcar were sown by the very factors which encouraged its growth.

In the next three years the final route extensions took place. That to Short Heath was opened on 23 June 1926, from Tyburn Road to Pype Hayes on 20 February 1927, and to Hall Green, again on reserved track, on 2 April 1928. The last extension came on 26 August 1928 when the Bordesley Green to Stuarts Road, Stechford, route along Bordesley Green East was completed.

Additionally, further route developments were taking place outside the city. The lease for the South Staffordshire Co, running between Colmore Row and Bilston via West Bromwich, expired in 1923, and from 1 April 1924 Birmingham Corporation trams ran to Wednesbury and to Dudley. On the latter route the Ryland aqueduct at Dudley Port was a severe limitation, in that the arched bridge precluded the operation of all the early top-covered cars in the 1-300 series together with all the ex-CBT cars.

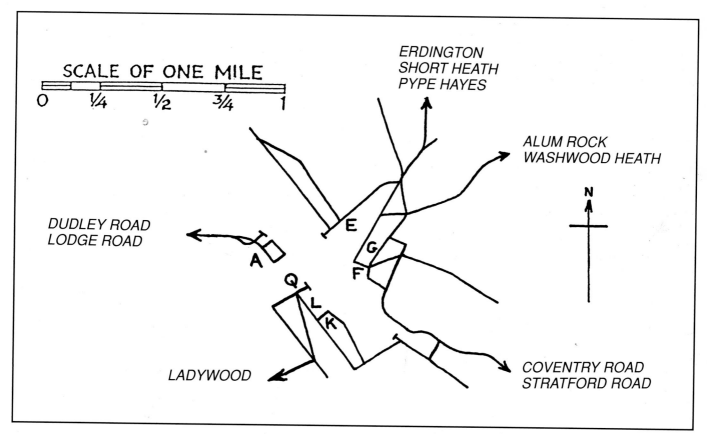

Termini in Birmingham city centre of the routes covered by this book.
A: Edmund Street (31, 32); E: Steelhouse Lane (1, 2, 63, 64, 78, 79); F: Martineau Street (3, 3X, 6, 7, 8, 9, 10); G: Dale End to Albert Street (13, 15, 17, 19, 44, 45, 56, 58, 82, 89, 91); K: Station Street (14, 16, 57); L: Station Street to Hill Street (18, 20, 21, 83); Q: Navigation Street (33, 34)

All of this, of course, required extra trams and, as can be seen from the fleet list on pages 98-99, from 1923 onwards totally enclosed bogie cars were built. They were based on the experiments undertaken with 342 and 347, which had received temporary permission from the Board of Trade to be enclosed, and the design of 347 was eventually used as the pattern for standard balcony designs.

The first of these totally enclosed trams were 25 cars built by the Midland Railway Carriage & Wagon Company (MRCW) at Washwood Heath, numbered 637-661, and most stayed at Miller Street depot for the whole of their working lives. Problems with delivery, however, led to MRCW never again tendering for any tramcar orders as financial penalty clauses were taken up by the Corporation; the original delivery deadline was wildly inaccurate and the cars entered service between October 1923 and January 1924.

The next class was built by Brush in two batches, 662-681 being delivered in March and April 1924 and 682-701 between December 1924 and February 1925. These trams had Dick, Kerr 40 hp motors. The next virtually identically bodied 702-731 Class had locally manufactured GEC motors of the same size.

In 1926 came further Brush-bodied trams, again on the now usual Electro-Magnetic Brake Co (EMB) Burnley bogies, but these were equipped with 63 hp Dick, Kerr motors and had EMB air-track brakes. These were the 732-761 Class, and they saw the standard Birmingham tramcar design develop a stage further. They were also the first class of trams to be fully upholstered with dark blue leather in each saloon, although the lower saloon seating was longitudinal.

In 1928 there was a further need to supplement the tramcar fleet after an extra 6½ route miles had been added with the Dudley, Oldbury and Smethwick takeover from the Birmingham and Midland system on 1 April. Once more the trams were ordered from Brush on the usual EMB Burnley bogies, but the cars had three major differences. First, the upper saloon had eight windows on each deck to give improved ventilation controllable by each passenger. Second, the cars had sixty-two upholstered transverse seats, and finally they were fitted with bow collectors for use on the Washwood Heath route. They were numbered 762-811. Older cars were then transferred from around the system to work on the newly acquired routes in the Oldbury area.

Between November 1928 and April 1929 were delivered what proved to be Birmingham's last class of tramcars, 812-841. These were similar to the previous class with 63 hp Dick, Kerr motors, but were built on Maley & Taunton Burnley bogies and M&T air wheel and track brakes. The contract for the bodies, however, broke new ground as they were ordered from Short Brothers of Rochester. Birmingham had been ordering bus bodies from them and must have been impressed by the quality of workmanship and the price, as Shorts tendered the lowest bid. These trams were delivered after the last route extensions and were allocated to Cotteridge depot where they took over the running of the Pershore Road route.

After this, although experimental lightweight cars 842 and 843 were delivered, there were to be no more new trams in Birmingham and virtually nothing in major route developments.

Within a year of the delivery of these two trams, the second route would be abandoned and the slow decline begin.

To be concluded in Volume 2

ABBREVIATIONS

BCT Birmingham Corporation Tramways. Changed to Birmingham Corporation Tramways & Omnibus Dept in 1927, then finally to Birmingham City Transport in November 1937.

BMMO Birmingham & Midland Motor Omnibus Co Ltd, Bearwood. The first major bus operator in the city; after 1914 it developed its own routes radiating from the city including routes into the Black Country.

BMT Birmingham & Midland Tramways Co Ltd. A BET tram operator that ran services in the Smethwick, Oldbury and Dudley area.

BRCW Birmingham Railway Carriage & Wagon Co Ltd, Smethwick. Supplied bus bodies to Birmingham Corporation.

BTH British Thompson-Houston Co Ltd, Rugby. Manufacturer of electrical equipment.

CBT City of Birmingham Tramways Co Ltd. Operator of horse, steam, cable, accumulator and electric tramways, formed on 29 September 1896 to take over the business of the Birmingham Central Tramways Co Ltd. Last routes in the city closed 31 December 1911.

DK Dick, Kerr & Co Ltd, Preston. The founding company that built electrical equipment but which diversified into tram and bus bodies.

EEC English Electric Co Ltd, Preston. Successor to UEC (see below).

EMB Electro-Mechanical Brake Co Ltd, West Bromwich. Manufacturer of electrical equipment, brakes, trucks and bogies from c1906-53. Other forms of engineering after that date.

ER&TCW Electric Railway & Tramway Carriage Works Ltd, Preston. Subsidiary of Dick, Kerr; became UEC (see below) 25 September 1905.

FEDD BMMO Front Entrance Double-Deck bus; standard Midland Red double-decker 1935-9.

GEC General Electric Co Ltd, Witton, Birmingham. Manufacturer of electric motors, controllers and components.

GWR Great Western Railway (not, contrary to some opinion, God's Wonderful Railway!).

LNWR London & North Western Railway

M&G Mountain & Gibson Ltd, Bury, Lancs. Manufacturer of trucks and bogies 1904-16

M&T Maley & Taunton Ltd, Wednesbury. Manufacturer of tramcar trucks and bogies, 1926-60.

MCCW Metropolitan-Cammell Carriage & Wagon Co Ltd, Birmingham. Bus, tram and railway carriage manufacturer from 1930 to 1989. Supplied the major part of Birmingham's bus bodies after 1933.

MOS Ministry of Supply, although to be accurate the Ministry of War Transport actually allocated vehicles during the Second World War.

MRCW Midland Railway-Carriage & Wagon Co Ltd, Saltley, Birmingham. Supplied BCT with 637 Class trams, but due to its failure to meet its own over-optimistic delivery dates, stopped tendering for tram orders. Taken over by MCCW group in 1929.

PW Permanent way (the permanent tracks as opposed to a contractor's tracks use during construction). A fleet of PW tramcars were kept at depots around Birmingham; they had their own number series, eg PW8.

REDD BMMO Rear Entrance Double-Deck bus from 1932 to 1934.

UEC United Electric Car Co. Merged with other companies 14 December 1918 to form EEC, Preston (see above).

Key to route maps
Reserved track on central island
Horse or steam tramways
City boundary

EARLY ABANDONMENTS

Coventry Road routes

THE Coventry Road routes shared with the Stratford Road services (see below) common city termini in High Street, for what became the 15 route, and Station Street, for the 16 route. They followed the same route out of the city as far as Bordesley, where the Coventry Road turned eastward underneath the Great Western Railway bridge and station. The development of the routes, however, followed a very different pattern from those of Stratford Road.

City of Birmingham Tramways Co (CBT) electric cars ran from the steam tram terminus at Small Heath Park across the city boundary at Hay Mills to Church Road, South Yardley, from 29 March 1904. CBT had run a steam tram service from the city centre to Small Heath Park from January 1886, but after reaching agreement with the Corporation, who relaid the track, a complete electric CBT service ran between Yardley and Station Street from 23 February 1905. This state of service was to last only until the CBT leases expired on New Year's Eve 1906,

after which the service was jointly worked with the Corporation.

Coventry Road (alternatively known as Arthur Street) depot was opened on 24 November 1905 for the Stechford routes, and the operation of the Coventry Road service began as part of the joint operation on 1 January 1907. During 1911 negotiations with the CBT company to purchase all of its operations in the newly enlarged Birmingham area had taken place and CBT operation on Coventry Road finished on 31 December of that year.

The Coventry Road route remained unaltered for the whole of its subsequent operational life. It was operated for most of that time by ex-Radial 71 Class cars or the smaller Brill trams from the 21 and 221 Classes.

After leaving Bordesley the cars climbed up Kingston Hill past Coventry Road, which at the time of opening had the largest capacity of any depot on the system, at 106 tramcars. At the junction of Cattell Road near the Birmingham City Football ground, the route turned right and passed through the linear Small Heath shopping centre which stretched over a half-mile section of the road.

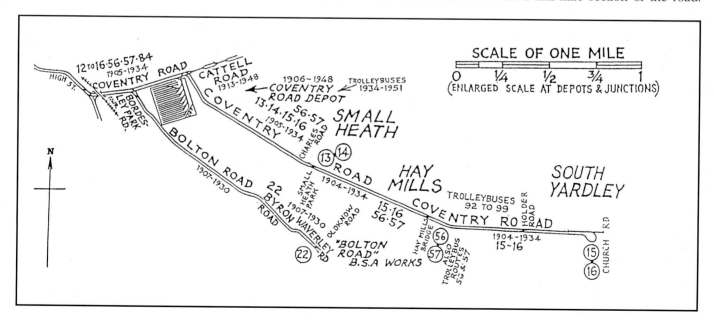

Coventry Road and Bolton Road routes

At the far end of these shops, at Charles Road opposite Small Heath Park, was the original steam tram terminus.

The route then descended past the last of the Victorian houses on Coventry Road whereupon it crossed the River Cole at Hay Mills. The flood plain of the river and its lower terraces were occupied by large factory units, and during the lifetime of the tram route the Singer Motor Works and the distant BSA factories could be seen. After the Hay Mills shops, the trams passed again into a residential area as they climbed through the erstwhile Yardley UDC to the terminus and CBT tram depot at Church Road opposite the Swan public house. Unusually for the Birmingham system, there was latterly a turning loop for the trams.

The only branch route was the Bolton Road 22 service which terminated in Waverley Road near the BSA factory. It, too, passed through an area of late-19th-century terraces before reaching the superior villas at the edge of Small Heath Park. The whole route was barely 1½ miles long and was never a financial success. It became the second route to be abandoned on 5 February 1930 and was replaced by one-man operated buses.

By 1932 the Coventry Road services were regarded as something of a financial burden. After much deliberation, not helped by the 1933 Salter Report on the taxation of public service vehicles, which would have been enormously damaging to the trolleybus lobby, the Corporation opted for trolleybuses. A fleet of 50 Leyland TTBD2 six-wheelers with MCCW bodies was ordered, which at the time was the largest trolleybus contract ever placed.

The tram routes along Coventry Road were abandoned on Saturday 6 January 1934, and on the following morning Coventry Road depot was operating a mixed fleet, with the remaining trams being used on the Stechford service.

Coventry Road, or Arthur Street, tram depot was opened on 24 November 1906 with a capacity for 106 cars. It was on a rather awkward site being on a steep hill and just beyond was the junction where the Stechford trams branched off Coventry Road at Cattell Road. After the opening of the trolleybus system on 7 January 1934, the tram fleet for the Stechford routes shared the accommodation at Arthur Street with the trolleybuses. Originally some 19 rows of tracks branched off the single entrance line, which can be seen in this 1951 view. Leyland TTBD2 trolleybus 30, (OC 1130) has passed the entrance after having negotiated one of the most complicated pieces of overhead wiring on the Birmingham system, and is continuing along the old tram route to the right of the Greenway Arms and its well-known horsetrough. The tram overhead for the Stechford route had carried straight on along Cattell Road to the left of the pub. This complicated overhead arrangement lasted until the Coventry Road trolleybus route was abandoned on 30 June 1951. *R. Wilson*

The United Electric Car Co (UEC) Radial car operating on the 16 route is possibly 140 and is certainly typical of Coventry Road's allocation of cars prior to the conversion; it is seen near the Yardley terminus on 22 October 1933. Photographs of tramcars working on Coventry Road are rare, and this particular one is of interest in that the print comes from a Gratispool paper negative. *F. Lloyd*

Standing just below the terminal loop at the Yardley terminus is car 86, which appears to be unloading its last passengers outside the Midland Bank before running around the loop opposite the Swan Hotel. It will then return to High Street in the city centre.

These 35 hp cars originally had a Mountain & Gibson Radial 8 ft 6 in trucks; they were designed to be self-centring after taking a curve, rather like a two-wheel bogie truck. Unfortunately, within a few years a combination of dust, mud and grease made the trucks' cornering characteristics somewhat idiosyncratic. The wheels would remain locked in the turning position or become rigid in the suspension. The result, as was found in Leeds with the later EMB Pivotal cars, was very poor riding quality - it was bumpy and produced side oscillating motions at anything above 12 mph. By the mid-1920s this car was one of 135 of the class to be re-equipped with Brush Peckham P35 trucks, and it remained in service until 30 September 1939 when it was sold for scrap after the Dudley Road abandonment. *S. J. Eades*

The City of Birmingham Tramways Co Ld (they actually abbreviated 'limited' in this unusual form) opened its electric tram route from Yardley to Small Heath on 29 March 1904 and joint working with Birmingham Corporation Tramways (BCT) into Birmingham began on the first day of 1907. The main stalwarts of the route in BCT days were the ex-Radial cars, and one of these, car 184, here negotiates the terminal loop, and apparently the bushes in the centre of the island, at the Yardley terminus in front of the Swan public house in 1933. This building replaced the old coaching inn of 1605 in the late 1890s. With its mock-Elizabethan styling, it dominated the whole area until 1967 when it was replaced with an anonymous structure whose only claim to fame was that it contained the longest bar counter in the world. *F. Lloyd*

The trolleybus turning circle at the Swan, Yardley, looking towards the city in about 1950. Metro-Cammell-bodied Leyland TB7 trolleybus 89 (FOK 89) is waiting to return to the city on the 94 route, and is facing the Midland Bank which appeared in the photograph of tram 86 on the previous page. The buses' turning circle occupied the turning loop which the 15 tram service used. This and the more famous Rednal loop on the Bristol Road route were the only ones on the tram system.

Today nothing is left of this scene. The bank and the Victorian terraces were swept away in the 1960s redevelopment scheme which involved the construction of an underpass to take the main A45 Coventry Road beneath the Outer Ring Road and the famous Outer Circle bus route. *R. T. Wilson*

Stratford Road Group

CBT STEAM trams had run since May 1885 as far as St Johns Road, Sparkhill, and were extended by about one mile to College Road, Springfield, in 1900, the last steam tram extension built in Birmingham. Electric trams replaced the steam tram service on 1 January 1907. The Stratford Road route was prepared for electrification by CBT before its lease expired, and the steam trams finished without ceremony on New Year's Eve 1906.

The main Stratford Road electric tram service had two city termini, Station Street, beside New Street Station, and High Street. In 1915 the route from the former terminus was numbered 18 and the latter 17. Although the 17 moved to Dale End and finally to Albert Street and the 18 moved round the corner to Hill Street, the basic concept that the routes served different areas of the city centre was maintained over the years.

On leaving the High Street area, the 17 tram route, together with the Coventry Road service 15 to Yardley, entered Moor Street and turned into the historical centre of Birmingham at the Bull Ring, whereupon it descended the steep hill into Digbeth.

The 18 route from Station Street went past the fruit and vegetable market in Moat Row and turned into Bradford Street, passing the city's main abattoir, before climbing up the hill to join the High Street service at Camp Hill.

Using the route common to the Coventry Road trams and one of the Stechford routes, as mentioned above, the trams passed through the mainly industrial areas of Deritend to the Coventry Road junction at Bordesley railway bridge. From here the Stratford Road cars, together with the Warwick Road 44 service from High Street, climbed up a steep rise to Camp Hill. This was so called after an incident in the Civil War in 1643 when Prince Rupert's army became involved in a small skirmish and used the hilltop site as their headquarters.

The cars then ran through the Victorian terraces and villas in Sparkbrook, travelling beneath the Midland Railway bridge at Henley Street, and immediately afterwards reached the junction with Kyotts Lake Road. Thereafter the Stoney Lane route branched off to the right at the start of the Sparkbrook shopping centre, and at the far end the Warwick Road route turned left, while the main route carried on up the hill to the Sparkhill shops passing the original steam tram terminus at St Johns Road. The route reached the 1900 steam tram terminus at the limit of the pre-First World War housing at College Road, but it was extended into the open country at Fox Hollies Road in May 1914. On 2 April 1928 a final extension was

The original terminus of the 44 Warwick Road tram route was about half a mile from Acocks Green at Broad Road. Car 132, one of the 71-220 Class of Mountain & Gibson Radial truck cars of 1906, is seen there in about 1918. The car displays the 'Birmingham Corporation Tramways' legal lettering on the rocker panel and has the wooden slipboard showing the somewhat vague destination of 'Acocks Green' below the lower saloon side windows. *R. T. Wilson collection*

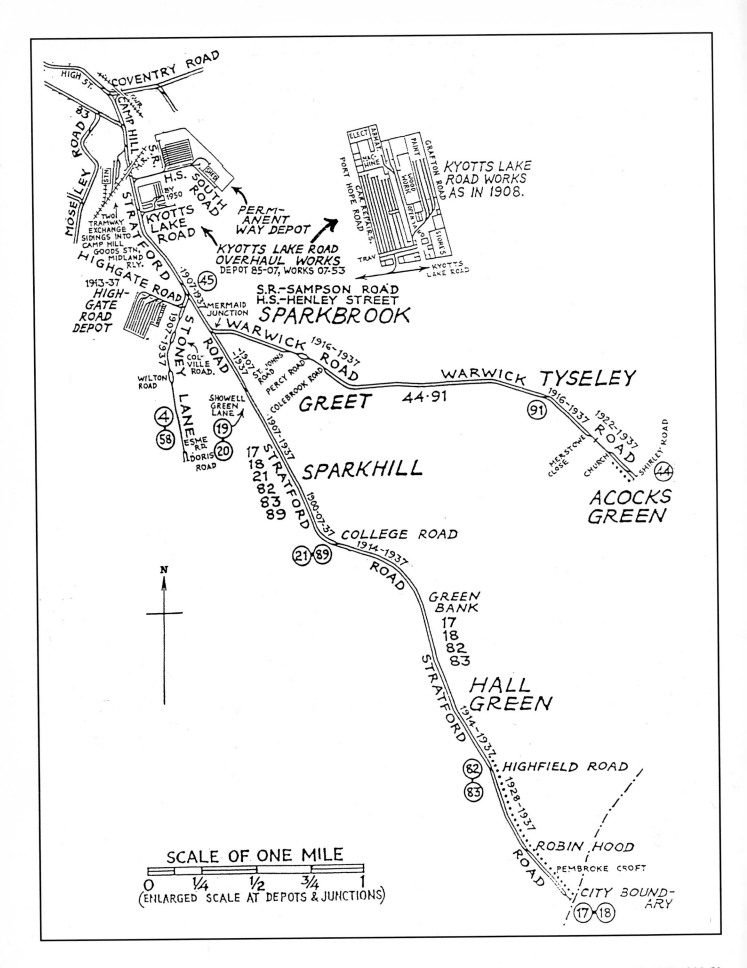

COVENTRY ROAD

HIGH ST.

83

MOSELEY ROAD

CAMP HILL

S.R.

STN.

BY 1950

H.S. SOUTH ROAD

KYOTTS LAKE ROAD

PERM-ANENT WAY DEPOT

KYOTTS LAKE ROAD OVERHAUL WORKS
DEPOT 85-07, WORKS 07-53

KYOTTS LAKE ROAD WORKS AS IN 1908.

ELECT. ARMAT. PAINT

MAC-HINE

PORT HOPE ROAD

CAR REPAIRS.

GRAFTON ROAD

WOOD WORK

OFFICE

STORES

TRAV.

KYOTTS LAKE ROAD

STRATFORD ROAD

1907-1937

45

MERMAID JUNCTION

1913-37 HIGH-GATE ROAD DEPOT

HIGHGATE ROAD

1907-1937

STONEY LANE

1907-1937

WILTON ROAD

4

58

SHOWELL GREEN LANE

19

20

ESME RD.
DORIS ROAD

COLVILLE ROAD.

1907-1937

ST. JOHNS ROAD

PERCY ROAD

COLEBROOK ROAD

WARWICK ROAD

1916-1937

S.R.—SAMPSON ROAD
H.S.—HENLEY STREET
SPARKBROOK

GREET

44.91

WARWICK

TYSELEY

91

1916-1937

ROAD

1922-1937

MERSTOWE CLOSE

CHURCH

SHIRLEY ROAD

44

ACOCKS GREEN

SPARKHILL

17
18
21
82
83
89

STRATFORD

1900-07-37

21 89

COLLEGE ROAD

1914-1937

ROAD

GREEN BANK

17
18
82
83

HALL GREEN

STRATFORD

1914-1937

82

83

HIGHFIELD ROAD

1928-1937

ROBIN HOOD

PEMBROKE CROFT

CITY BOUND-ARY

17 18

N

SCALE OF ONE MILE

0   ¼   ½   ¾   1

(ENLARGED SCALE AT DEPOTS & JUNCTIONS)

TWO TRAMWAY EXCHANGE SIDINGS INTO CAMP HILL GOODS STN, MIDLAND RLY.

made to the city boundary along a splendid piece of reserved track. This, in fact, proved to be the penultimate main-line route extension in the city's tramway system and served the huge inter-war suburban developments in Hall Green.

In later years Highgate Road depot at Sparkbrook operated some 40 hp bogie cars from the 512 Class along Stratford Road although continuing to use the earlier 21 Class, the ex-Radial four-wheelers and the 301 Class.

As already mentioned, the Stratford Road group of routes had one major branch along Warwick Road which left Stratford Road at the Mermaid public house, Sparkbrook. It ran through the small 1880s shopping centre at Greet and climbed up to Tyseley, passing the entrance to the Great Western Railway's motive power depot. This marked the only shortworking on the route, numbered 91, the main 44 route carrying on to Acocks Green.

The original terminus was at Broad Lane; although the track along Warwick Road had been laid for about two years, because of track clearance problems the route was not opened until 2 February 1916. It was finally extended

the last half mile into Acocks Green in October 1922. The original terminus was also altered a few years later from adjacent to the Westley Road junction to the middle of the large traffic island which was built in the centre of Acocks Green 'village'.

The second Stratford Road branch, along Stoney Lane, was opened at the same time as the conversion from steam tram operation in 1907. This was the 4 route and was one of the shortest branch routes on the Birmingham system, being barely three-quarters of a mile long.

Originally the Stratford Road routes were partially operated from the old CBT headquarters at Kyotts Lake Road, but within a year of the introduction of electric tramcars 'The Lake' became the main repair works for the whole system. The Stratford Road and Stoney Lane routes were then operated by Coventry Road depot until Monday 24 November 1913. Upon the opening of Highgate Road depot, both services and the later Warwick Road route ran from this depot until the closure of the Stratford Road group when car 564 was finally pulled into the depot by enthusiasts in the early hours of 6 January 1937.

Left **Stratford Road and Warwick Road routes**

Above **The Acocks Green route along Warwick Road to Broad Road was opened on 2 February 1916, being extended to Acocks Green 'village' in October 1922. Tram 245, a 1908 UEC**

former open-topper, stands at the new terminus on 3 May 1923. **The Carnegie-funded library at Acocks Green, the New Inns public house and the Warwick Cinema had yet been built, and the rural nature of the suburb could still be seen.** *Birmingham Public Works Dept*

The Birmingham electric tramcar system suffered from having no direct route across the city centre and a scattering of termini just outside the main shopping area. Perhaps the most remote of these was Station Street which was on the south side of New Street Station, where car 497 stands on the site of the triangular track junction, just masking the Station Street cafe. Car 497 was ex-CBT 236 and had been built by the Brush Company of Loughborough in late 1904, being purchased in 1912 by BCT. When this photograph was taken in 1933, 497, as it had been renumbered, had been transformed from a green-and-cream-liveried open-topper to a 35 hp tram with platform vestibules and top covers. It is on the 83 route shortworking from Station Street to Highfield Road, Hall Green, on the Stratford Road route.

Further down Station Street was the famous Birmingham Repertory Theatre which opened on 15 February 1913 with a production of Shakespeare's 'Twelfth Night'. *J. Cull*

The bustling Victorian shopping centres of Sparkhill and Sparkbrook on Stratford Road had been developed after the 1876 building byelaws had come into effect. The result was a swathe of terraced and tunnel-backed housing stretching from Highgate through Sparkbrook to Small Heath. UEC ex-Radial car 163 stands in Stoney Lane just south-west of the junction with Stratford Road in late 1936. The shops and houses were by then some 50 years old and the days of the tram were already numbered. A 1936 Daimler COG5 bus flashes by along Stratford Road in the distance - the trams could not compete with the up-to-date buses which worked the newer suburban developments not served by trams. By 5 January 1937 the trams had gone and the nearby Highgate Road depot was converted to bus operation. *R. T. Wilson*

Birmingham Corporation Tramways ordered 150 cars from Dick, Kerr & Co Ltd which were delivered between August 1906 and March 1907 with UEC-built 52-seater bodies. They were 16 ft 0½ in high, which enabled them to pass beneath Stratford Road and Coventry Road railway bridges; this 71-220 Class, therefore, became the early 'backbone' of the tramway fleet. Car 147 stands at the College Road terminus in Stratford Road early in 1907, not long after the January opening. These Victorian terraces marked a temporary halt in the building of houses along Stratford Road, and the late Edwardian Hall Green Parade shops were only reached in May 1914 when the trams went to Fox Hollies Road,

which, at that time, was still an area of green fields. *BCT*

The 71-220 Class was finally withdrawn on 30 September 1939 after the closure of the Oldbury, Smethwick and Dudley lines. Car 147 saw service on the last day and was supposedly broken up at West Smethwick depot in April 1940. However, here are the remains of the lower saloon of the tram, having been used as a motorcycle repair shed beside the main A45 Coventry Road near Birmingham Airport. This was all that was left of the tram in July 1986, but inside some of the gilt lettering, including the fleet number, could still be seen. *D. R. Harvey*

Above The reserved track from Fox Hollies Road to the city boundary at Shirley was never really exploited by BCT, opening on 2 April 1928 and closing on 5 January 1937. During that period it was partially operated by Highgate Road's 71-220 Class ex-Radial type four-wheelers which dated from the 1906-07 period. Car 174, seen here on the 18 route, was retrucked with a Brush-built Peckham unit in the mid-1920s. The 1936 Morris Eight car shows that this view was taken during the last year of operation.

Below Car 99, working the 17 route to High Street, waits at the Hall Green terminus before returning to the city. This car entered service in 1906 and was initially allocated to Washwood Heath depot before being transferred to Highgate Road depot in the 1920s. It was finally broken up in September 1939 after the closure of the West Smethwick routes. *Both W. A. Camwell*

LADYWOOD AND LODGE ROAD ROUTES

Ladywood

THE Ladywood 33 route served the inner areas of Birmingham, passing through some of the oldest 19th-century back-to-back houses, as well as through areas of industry. The 2½-mile route, opened on 17 October 1906, took a somewhat devious route from Navigation Street in the city centre to the junction of Icknield Port Road and Dudley Road, it terminated only about 1½ miles from where it started. It was always operated by Rosebery Street depot which was some half a mile citywards from the terminus at Dudley Road.

The original city terminus of the route was at the Queens Hotel end of Navigation Street, but in 1929 this was moved to where the Bristol Road group of routes began at the Suffolk Street end of the same street. From its opening until 1915 the route was identified on the trams by the stencil letter `L'.

The cars left the city centre following the Bristol Road routes for the length of John Bright Street until, on reaching the Horsefair, they crossed the inbound Bristol Road cars and climbed Holloway Head and into Bath Row, passing some very poor quality housing on the hill and St

Thomas's Church; everything but the spire of this 18th-century church was destroyed in an air raid.

After passing Davenport's Brewery and the Accident Hospital, the cars turned into Islington Row. The whole of this area was cleared in the 1950s and renamed Lee Bank, but for the latter years of the trams' involvement in public transport in the area, these were amongst the worst slum properties in the city.

At Five Ways the 34 route turned left and westwards towards the distant Kings Head terminus at Bearwood, but the Ladywood cars continued northwards past the Children's Hospital in Ladywood Road, again passing some early Victorian three-storied courtyard housing, before reaching Chamberlain Gardens at the corner of Monument Road. Here a remnant of the Regency housing of Edgbaston stood as a reminder of the time when nearby Ivy Bush was one of the most prosperous 19th-century areas in Birmingham.

The tram route turned right into Monument Road, then left into Icknield Port Road at the Municipal Bank. It then descended in a straight line into an area of factories for about a quarter of a mile, before beginning to climb again past factories towards some mid-19th-century three-sto-

The 33 route to Ladywood left the Navigation Street terminus via John Bright Street, then turned across the Horsefair and up the steep hill of Holloway Head. Car 735 is one of the Electro-Magnetic Brake Co (EMB) bogie air-brake cars of 1926, with a Brush 63-seat body.

The pointsman has reset the junction in Suffolk Street under the watchful eye of the Inspector as the tram turns into Holloway Head on Sunday 31 March 1940 on a wrong-line working probably caused by track maintenance. Behind is car 837 on the 36 route to Cotteridge.

Peterson's Rubber Co shop, on the corner of Holloway Head and Suffolk Street, was destroyed in the bombing of 24-25 October 1940, one of the first serious nights of bombing which Birmingham suffered during the Second World War.
D. Clayton

ried terraces; this depressing landscape on the western side of the road successfully hid the tree-lined Rotton Park Reservoir. On this straight section of the route there were three passing loops.

There was a section of double track at the terminus which led into the left-handed curve that joined Dudley Road, but because of the narrowness of Icknield Port Road, cars stood in the single-track section. This of course meant that any outbound tram had to wait in the Gillott

Road loop at the top of the Icknield Port Road hill until the terminus was cleared. Trams on depot workings from Rosebery Street could only reach Icknield Port Road by running beyond the junction on Dudley Road, then reversing to the start of the 33 route.

The route was originally operated by four-wheelers, but after 1926 Rosebery Street depot used the air-braked bogie trams from the 732 Class. The service was withdrawn on 30 August 1947.

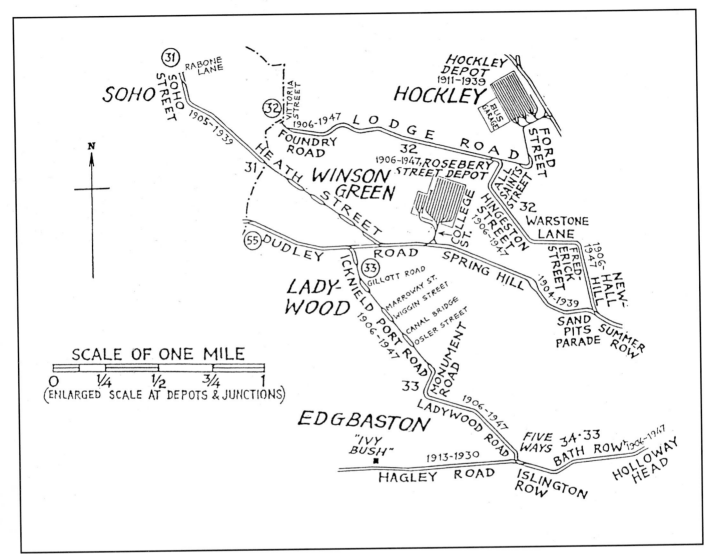

Ladywood and Lodge Road routes

The Ladywood trams passed along Islington Row to the junction of Broad Street and Five Ways. On 28 August 1947 car 733, one of the 732-761 Class, crosses the junction in front of Lloyds Bank and the Art Deco shops at the top of Islington Row before passing into Ladywood Road. These bogie cars were synonymous with the 33 route and worked from Rosebery Street depot until it closed with the abandonment of the Ladywood route on 31 August 1947. *L. W. Perkins*

BIRMINGHAM TRAMS 1933-53

After passing the famous Birmingham Children's Hospital in Ladywood Road, the trams arrived at the junction with Monument Road, passing the now long since demolished premises of Thomas Furber & Sons, the undertakers who established their business as long ago as 1868. Their premises, seen on the left of this 1947 view, lay opposite the Chamberlain Gardens recreation area, behind the tram. These were opened by the local Member of Parliament, Neville Chamberlain, on 28 June 1924.

This photograph of car 754 was taken within a few months of the closure of the 33 route, and the last remnants of wartime restrictions were evident - the lamp-posts still have blackout markings and there is a complete lack of cars as petrol rationing was still in force at this time. Car 754 was uniquely fitted with a removable window at each balcony end in order to gain access to the trolley-pole. *J. S. Webb*

On a dark, dismal day in 1947, car 740 has just turned out of Monument Road into Icknield Port Road. The Birmingham Municipal Bank to the right of the tram was typical of the smaller branches opened in the years after the First World War; it was opened by the Lord Mayor, a Miss Williams, on 14 June 1924.

The West Bromwich-registered two-door Morris Eight saloon was almost new when this view was taken. The queue of intending passengers spilling into the roadway would not be possible with today's traffic. *D. R. Harvey collection*

Above 'Post it to Vernons, the pools you can trust' sits a little uncomfortably on the advertising hoarding next to the entreaties to join the Territorial Army. Car 733, one of the EMB air-brake cars, rattles through the first of the three passing loops in Icknield Port Road, near the Henry Wiggins wire factory, on its way to the terminus in August 1947. Most people seem oblivious to the tram, still in its prewar livery, the advertisements and the nearly new Morris Eight four-door saloon. *W. A. Camwell*

Below The middle passing loop in the 33 route in Icknield Port Road was at the Belle View public house. This Ansells house has survived, but virtually all the houses have since been demolished; the large factory complexes behind the two trams are also still there today. On the right is car 747, outward bound from the city centre to the terminus about half a mile away, passing inbound car 740 during the last few weeks of operation. This latter tram is in the prewar lined-out livery, the somewhat faded grandeur of which does not do it justice when compared to the recently repainted 747. *J. S. Webb*

The Dick, Kerr DK30/1L 63 hp motors of 738, one of the 732-761 Class, were wasted in the confines of deepest Victorian Ladywood. It is 1947 and the tram has been repainted into the simpler postwar livery, though still retaining the prewar fleet numbers. Some of the three-storied terrace houses in Icknield Port Road had, by this time, been converted to shops, but even the sunshine could do no more than temporarily brighten up the already run-down cobbled street. *W. A. Camwell*

The Ladywood terminus stopped short of Dudley Road although the track was linked so that depot journeys to Rosebery Street could take place. The loop was not actually used as the terminus because two trams parked there would have occupied most of the road space; it was mainly used to gain access from Icknield Port Road into Dudley Road. This manoeuvre was done by wrong line running out of the last loop in Icknield Port Road, so gaining the inbound Dudley Road track back to the depot.

Car 633 stands just beyond the terminal loop, with a Dudley Road 71-220 Class car passing in the distance. It was one of 50 trams built in 1920 by Brush with 37 hp motors and open balconies. The by now totally enclosed tramcar was one of only 15 of the 587-636 Class to survive until the final closure of the system, and was finally broken up in July 1953. *W. A. Camwell*

Lodge Road

COMPETING with the famous 'Chinese Railway' routes in Balsall Heath for being the most tortuous on the BCT system, Lodge Road also had the added problem of being one of the hilliest. The nature of the route and the fact that a fatal accident occurred on 1 October 1907 in Warstone Lane involving car 22, resulted in Lodge Road always being worked by the smallest four-wheel trams in the fleet. A total of 54 cars from the 21-70 and the 221-300 Classes were equipped with the Maley track brake in 1909 and 1910 as a response to the accident and some were specifically allocated to the Lodge Road route. In 1926 15 of these small Brill-Maley cars were fitted with new bow collectors and up to 18 trams in all were fitted with this method of current collection exclusively for the Lodge Road route.

The route itself started beneath the pedestrian bridge in Edmund Street between the Council House and its later Edwardian extension. On leaving the terminus, the route turned into Congreve Street and continued into Summer Row where it met the inbound cars. These turned into Great Charles Street and unloaded in Edmund Street, effectively giving all the Dudley Road group of routes a turning loop around the city's administrative buildings.

The outbound cars followed the Dudley Road routes as far as Newhall Hill where they turned right up the steep hill into the Jewellery Quarter.

After passing along Frederick Street, with its 19th-century workshops and converted houses, the tram route turned left at the Chamberlain Clock and descended Warstone Hill. Here it passed Warstone Lane cemetery which is one of the oldest burial grounds in Birmingham. At the bottom of the hill the cars passed the famous Birmingham Mint before crossing Icknield Street and the Inner Circle bus route. The route then climbed Hingeston Street and turned right over the GWR railway line near Hockley Goods Station.

The 32 route then turned left and climbed Lodge Road, with terraced houses to the right and the mid-19th-century All Saints Hospital and Winson Green Prison to the left. On reaching Winson Green Road, the trams crossed the Outer Circle bus route and descended Foundry Road, passing an area of late Victorian tunnel-back terraces before reaching the terminus.

The Lodge Road route was unique in the Birmingham tram system in that it started and finished beneath bridges - at the outer terminus this was a railway bridge at the city boundary. The trams reversed at a terminal stub cross-over opposite the Railway Inn.

The Lodge Road route should have been withdrawn at the same time as the rest of the Dudley Road tram services, but was reprieved for the duration of the Second World War and was not abandoned until 29 March 1947.

The sandbags stacked up in Edmund Street alongside Gas Hall in the Council House extension of 1913 are the most tangible evidence that the Second World War had broken out. In fact, this is the last day of operation of the Dudley Road routes, 30 September 1939. The abandonment of these routes, on which the leading car, 209, is running, proceeded despite the hostilities, and was due to the poor state of the track beyond the city boundary.

The second car is one of the Brill 21E truck cars of 1906 which had been fitted with the Maley magnetic track brake after three years service, and equipped with bow collectors in 1924. It is working the 16-minute journey to Lodge Road on the 32 route. *L. W. Perkins*

Car 50 stands beneath the Council House extension bridge in August 1946. It is in the wartime grey livery and was, in fact, the only one of the seventeen Brill-Maley cars retained after 1939 to be painted grey; it was never repainted back into normal livery.

This part of Edmund Street is now pedestrianised and a small length of track has been laid down to add a touch of nostalgia to the ever-changing face of Birmingham's city centre. *D. R. Harvey collection*

The tortuous curves of the Lodge Road route were always a feature and led to its nickname of 'The Dipper'. The 32 route was also quite hilly, the steepest part being Newhall Hill, which led from the Dudley Road routes at Sandpits Parade up to Warstone Lane clock at the heart of the Jewellery Quarter in Hockley. The lantern-lit King Edward VI public house on the left and the late Victorian Buckingham Buildings factory on the right guard the entrance to Newhall Hill as Brill-Maley car 49 starts to ascend in this early postwar view. *G. F. Skipp*

At the top of Warstone Lane is the famous Birmingham Jewellery Quarter. This area has been developed continuously since the 18th century and is a mixture of impressive purpose-built works and converted houses with rear workshops down entries and narrow passages. The centre of the Jewellery Quarter is the Chamberlain Clock at the junction of Vyse Street and Warstone Lane. It is a cast iron memorial to Joseph Chamberlain's visit to South Africa in 1903; unveiled by his wife, Mary, on 30 January 1904, it was restored in the late 1980s to its ornately painted best.

Car 222 approaches the clock before turning left into Warstone Lane. It will then descend the hill carefully, as this was the site of the 1 October 1907 accident when car 22, basically of the same type as 222 but in original open-top condition, overturned with the loss of two lives. *Newman College collection*

The driver of car 67 glances at the photographer as his tram approaches the Frederick Street junction in Warstone Lane on 19 April 1939. The extreme shortness of the six-foot Brill truck with its Maley track brake can be noted beneath this 27 ft 6 in long tram.

Sutton's ironmongers and the tobacconist behind the tram were typical of the small shops in prewar Birmingham and belong to a tradition of retailing which has since largely been replaced by superstores and multi-national companies. In the Jewellery Quarter only the small shops selling locally wrought jewellery have survived. *L. W. Perkins*

The short-wheelbase Brill-Maley cars equipped with Fischer bow collectors were well suited to the twists and turns of the Lodge Road route. Although originally intended to be withdrawn in 1939, the war delayed the abandonment, so these 48-seater cars continued to work through the Jewellery Quarter, Hockley and Winson Green until 30 March 1947.

Car 61 has been parked on the disused spur in Lodge Road on 30 June 1940 after breaking an axle. Careful examination reveals that the rear axle has been placed on a temporary truck which will enable the car to be towed back to Rosebery Street depot. The car has been fitted with wartime headlight masks and has had its fender painted white, but despite wartime restrictions and privations, the gold lining and the paintwork sparkle in the early summer sunshine. *D. Clayton*

The sharp curves of the 32 route can be appreciated in this pre-war view, again featuring car 61, taken in Lodge Road on 29 July 1939. The abandoned single line in the foreground had been the link between Rosebery Street and Hockley tram depots, but the latter had been converted to bus operation on 1 April 1939.

The tram is passing a small row of shops; glimpsed beyond it is a Bradford's electric bread van, while on the right is a Fordson van owned by the famous butchers Marsh & Baxter. An advertisement for Kodak film on the left belies the fact that this was only five weeks before the outbreak of the Second World War, and that soon such luxuries would be a thing of the past. *H. B. Priestley*

Rosebery Street depot was opened on 14 April 1906 and was responsible for all Birmingham Corporation routes along the Dudley Road. It also worked the Hagley Road, Ladywood and, at various times, the Lodge Road routes. When the Birmingham and District lease expired on 31 March 1928, some workings were shared with the newly acquired West Smethwick depot. The capacity of the depot was 85 cars, and of those typically about fifteen large bogie cars were required for the Ladywood route. The remainder were of three types: the small three-windowed Brill-Maley trams such as cars 53 and 255, seen here on the left, were used for the Lodge Road route; the second type was the ex-Radial cars such as 124, which worked along the main Dudley Road; and the third was as car 466, an ex-Company car, formerly numbered 206, which had been acquired in 1911 and was a CBT 'Aston' type built in 1904 as an open-top, open-vestibuled car.

This view, taken on 29 March 1939, shows four of the 12 roads in the depot. Only cars 53 and 255 would survive the Second World War. *W. A. Camwell*

As it climbed Lodge Road, the 32 route passed a series of fairly grim reminders of Victorian social history. The first was the City Fever Hospital, established in 1875 so that more smallpox and scarlet fever victims could be isolated. The trams then passed the architecturally impressive but sobering Borough Lunatic Asylum; built in the style of a Tudor mansion and opened in 1850, it is now All Saints Hospital. At the top of Lodge Road was the gaol, built like a toy fortress, castellated and round-arched, which later became HM Prison Winson Green. It was designed in 1849 by D. R. Hill, the same architect who was responsible for the asylum.

Car 53 lets off passengers near the prison in 1946. It will next cross Winson Green Road and go down Foundry Road to the terminus less than a quarter of a mile away. *J. S. Webb*

The terminus of the Lodge Road route at Foundry Road lay within a triangle of railway bridges formed by the London & North Western Railway main line to Wolverhampton and the Soho and Perry Barr branch line, one of whose bridges is seen behind Brill-Maley car 255. This prewar view shows the neat appearance of these small former open-toppers. Although among the oldest trams in the BCT fleet, they did have the most modern method of current collection; unfortunately their short 6-foot wheelbase trucks produced a hard 'tail-wagging' ride, and the longitudinal wooden seats in the lower saloon did not exactly make the passengers feel comfortable. *D. R. Harvey collection*

BIRMINGHAM TRAMS 1933-53

The Foundry Road terminus of the 32 route was not one of the most picturesque settings in Birmingham. On 15 August 1939 car 260 waits at the Railway Inn terminus; to the left of the Bundy clock is the ex-LNWR railway embankment near Soho South junction. On the other side of the embankment, and beyond the Birmingham & Wolverhampton Canal less than a quarter of a mile away, was the 31 tram route which ran parallel to the railway and canal along Heath Street and terminated at Soho Station. Unlike the 32 route, the Soho route was abandoned on 30 September 1939. *L. W. Perkins*

The Hillman car is parked outside the Railway Inn as, perhaps, its driver enjoys the delights of the locally brewed Mitchells & Butlers beer. Car 61 stands beneath the railway embankment next to the Bundy clock, which recorded departure times on a card roll when the driver turned a key beneath the clock face. This view, taken on a rather overcast 29 July 1939, shows evocatively the simple stub terminal line in this rather depressing industrial environment. The advertising hoardings extol the virtues of healthy living by drinking milk, smoking Wills's 'Star' cigarettes - only 9d for 20 - and 'Persil whiteness'. *H. B. Priestley*

WASHWOOD HEATH ROUTES

Washwood Heath

THE 4½-mile run to Washwood Heath on the 10 route to some extent epitomised the variations in Birmingham's urban landscape during its journey via Saltley to the Fox and Goose. The route was opened on 2 May 1907 and the service was initially operated by 71 Class cars and some of the smaller open-topped 21 and 221 Classes from Washwood Heath depot.

The 10 route, which was lettered 'W' until 1915, started in Martineau Street with the Alum Rock, Nechells, Witton and Perry Barr routes. Martineau Street was probably the city terminus nearest to the main shopping streets, and the routes that used it gave their passengers certain advantages regarding walking distances although this was somewhat negated by the terminus not having any covered tram stops.

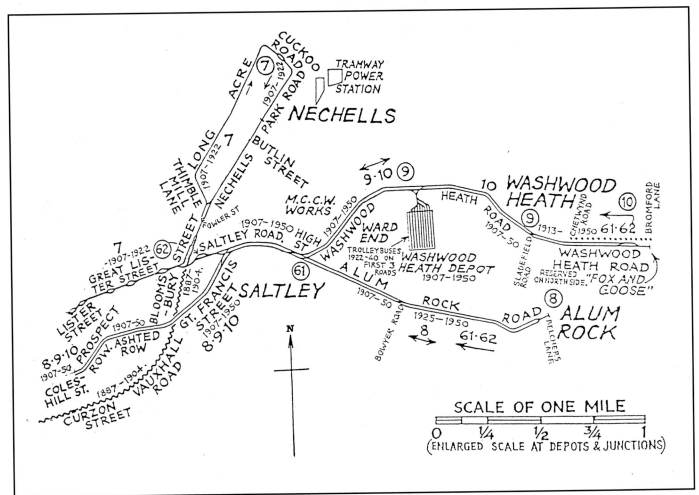

Washwood Heath, Alum Rock and Nechells routes

On leaving the third loading stand from the top of Martineau Street, the trams turned into Corporation Street passing *en route* some of the largest and most popular shops in the city centre. The route passed the Old Square, where Newbury's department store stood, later replaced by Lewis's, then proceeded along Corporation Street until they reached the junction with John Watt Street. Here, in later years, because of problems with trams with trolley poles at junctions designed for bow-collector operation, 301 Class cars would have to be de-poled before proceeding out of the city beyond this point.

The whole of Corporation Street became the subject of a police review of traffic congestion in the city centre in 1931, which resulted in the development of Birmingham's famous (or infamous) one-way system which started in 1933. The result, as far as all the Martineau Street routes, including the Washwood Heath services, were concerned, was that from Bull Street to the Old Square the trams ran against the one-way system on their outward journey.

On reaching the bottom of James Watt Street the trams turned across the inbound trams from Witton coming along Stafford Street. The Washwood Heath services then ran through Ashted, a once prosperous Regency area, whose early wealth had been overtaken by the rapid mid-19th-century expansion of industrial Birmingham: Coleshill Street, Prospect Row and Ashted Row were a mixture of terraces, courtyards and some of the first municipal housing built in the 19th century. From Great Francis Street to Saltley Road were houses that would be swept away under one of Birmingham's first comprehensive urban renewal plans.

At Saltley Road the landscape changed dramatically as the Rea Valley was crossed. Here were numerous railway sidings, the Birmingham & Warwick Junction canal and a mixture of small workshops and large factories, all bound together by the permeating smell from Saltley Gas Works. After crossing Saltley Viaduct over the flat flood plain,

High Street, Saltley, and the Gate public house were reached.

The Gate marked the junction where the Alum Rock route carried straight on through the main Saltley shopping centre. The 10 route, however, turned left into Washwood Heath Road and climbed through a residential area until the tram depot just after a small shopping area at Aston Church Road. The route then dropped down a steep hill to Ward End Park and the Morris motor works before curving round the edge of the park to the original terminus at Sladefield Road, in another shopping area.

A route extension left Sladefield Road as the 9 short-working when, on 20 December 1913, the new three-quarters of a mile section was opened to the Fox & Goose public house at Bromford Lane. This enabled the route to serve the proposed housing developments near the new terminus, most of which was not in fact built until after the First World War. An unusual feature of part of this last extension was the side reservation from Chetwynd Road to the terminus.

This route and Alum Rock were selected for conversion to bow collector operation after September 1928 when the 762-811 Class of EMB air-brake cars was allocated to Washwood Heath. These trams ran the Washwood Heath route, supported by a few older four-wheelers, until the trams were replaced by buses on 1 October 1950.

It is worth noting that, like Coventry Road depot, Washwood Heath also operated trolleybuses and motor buses; in this case they were for the Nechells route which had been the first tram-replacement trolleybus route in Britain, in November 1922. The trolleybuses ran from the depot to Bloomsbury Street, Saltley, using the positive tram overhead and a skate on the rail for the return current. On 1 October 1940 the route was abandoned because these 'skate-operated' depot journeys produced a good deal of arcing, causing a lot of sparking to take place which was not considered conducive to good blackout, especially during air raids.

Although Martineau Street disappeared from the face of Birmingham's city centre in October 1960, with Kunzle's cakeshop and the tobacconists with the Abdullah cigarette advertisement at the top end it seemed to epitomise the late Victorian civic pride for which the Martineau family was noted - three generations of Martineaus were Mayors or Lord Mayors of the city. Martineau Street linked High Street with Corporation Street and it was from here that the Washwood Heath and Alum Rock cars started. Car 769 stands just below the 8 route stand in 1950 while a family alights from the tram on the offside, a practice which was positively encouraged at city loop termini, so that loading could start immediately. *D. R. Harvey collection*

By mid-1950 the Alum Rock routes were being prepared for abandonment. They were a mixture of street track and, in the case of the Washwood Heath route, an unusual piece of reserved track which involved running on one side of the road! In Martineau Street and throughout the city centre kerb loading was standard practice. Car 773, one of the 1928 EMB airbrake cars, is working the Alum Rock 8 route. It is standing behind bus 1737, a 1948 Leyland 'Titan' PD2/1 with a Brush H30/24R body. This is working the 39 route to Witton via Aston Cross and passing Villa Park, home of Aston Villa FC. In the distance, in Corporation Street, is a Park Royal-bodied wartime bus. *A. B. Cross*

This view of a really bustling scene in April 1949 shows, besides car 769 on the 10 route, a newly repainted Leyland TTBD2 six-wheel trolleybus turning out of Carrs Lane. It is passing the News Theatre that had been opened on 18 January 1932 by Neville Chamberlain, who was at that time Chancellor of the Exchequer. The Waverley Hotel beside it was an Ansells public house on the small triangular site formed by High Street, New Meeting Street and Albert Street, and has the impedimenta of clock and lantern-style light adorning its facade; in front of it stands a policeman on point duty. Albert Street, into which the trolleybus will turn, contained the terminus of some of the Moseley Road trams, Stechford trams and the Coventry Road trolleybuses, as well as Birmingham's famous 'Beehive' store.

To the left of the tram, at this six-way junction, is the lower part of Bull Street with the tobacconist on the rounded corner. *F. Lloyd Jones*

Turning in front of the small island, which contained a gentlemen's subterranean toilet, from Dale End into Martineau Street is car 766. This tram, delivered new to Washwood Heath depot in 1928 to replace that depot's allocation of ex-Radial cars, was one of the Brush-built air-brake cars that ran with bow collectors until the closure of the Washwood Heath route on 30 September 1950. In common with the other 48 cars that survived the Second World War, it was transferred to Selly Oak depot. The destination number blind has an unusually large '0' as part of the route number 10. Tram 766 was withdrawn about two months before the rest of the class, in May 1952, because of a defective truck.

One of Perry Barr garage's Leyland 'Titan' PD2/1s of the 1656-1755 Class built in 1948 with Brush bodies is following the tram around into Martineau Street on the 33 bus route from Kingstanding. *D. R. Harvey collection*

A Rover car travels along a nearly deserted Corporation Street with only a distant Midland Red wartime Daimler CWA6 and tramcar 799 on the 8 route for company. The tram route actually travelled against the one-way traffic flow here as it passed, on its left, Lewis's department store, originally opened in 1885 and rebuilt in 1927. Immediately beyond the two women on the left is the Old Square. This had been the site of the medieval Hospital of St Thomas the Martyr, known more commonly as 'The Priory', and that name survives today in the name Priory Queensway, which is part of the Inner Ring Road. The Georgian buildings of the Old Square were demolished with the cutting of the 'Parisian Boulevard' in the 1880s which Corporation Street was intended to become.

In the distance is the slim, square tower of the Methodist Central Hall which was completed in 1903. It was built to the designs of Ewan and James Harper in a curious mixture of late Gothic style mixed with Renaissance detail. To the right of the tram is Kings Hall which was opened in 1907 as a vaudeville theatre, but was quickly converted to a cinema. This venture also failed and it closed in 1920 after showing a film entitled 'The Market of Souls' starring Dorothy Dalton. Next door to the Kings Hall, away from the road junction, was the Grand Theatre which closed in May 1933 also after being converted into a cinema. *R. T. Wilson*

Car 357 of the 301 Class turns into James Watt Street from Corporation Street on the Washwood Heath route. These UEC 52-seater trams were built in 1911, mounted on Preston 'flexible axle' 7 ft 6 in swing-yoke trucks, and fitted with Dick, Kerr DKBA 40 hp motors; they were to give up to 39 years of service. Car 357 had been transferred from Coventry Road depot in October 1948 and was to become the official last car on the 10 route on the evening of Saturday 30 September 1950, being one of the cars that achieved about 1,170,000 miles in service. By this time they were some of the last open-balconied trams running on a narrow gauge system in the country. They were also unusual for Washwood Heath's allocation in that they were fitted with trolley poles rather than bow collectors. *R. T. Wilson*

James Watt Street hardly exists today, with only a short length of the buildings at the top of the hill on the right still remaining. A rather shabby car 769 working the 8 route to Alum Rock descends the hill to the junction with Stafford Street and Dale End on a warm summer's day, 7 June 1950. It carries a Barber's Teas advertisement on the balcony panel; Barbers were a local firm, established in 1797, and based in Pershore Street. Their quarter-pound packets of tea contained picture cards which were more collectable than the tea! Barbers were taken over by Twinings in about 1961. *F. Lloyd*

Today Coleshill Street, from which car 357 has just emerged, is, like James Watt Street, but a memory. Parts of the campus of Aston University now cover this site, and the Victorian shops and warehouses have all been razed to the ground, including Gaskell & Chambers who supplied public houses with bar pump engines. Also demolished was James' Stores with its splendid gable-end advertisement.

Car 766 is coming into the city on the 8 route on 10 May 1950. All the 762-811 Class were supplied with Fischer bow collectors from new, and although successful in that dewirements became a rarity and faster running was therefore possible, they did produce excessive wear on the overhead wire if the bow was not lubricated. This factor precluded the extension of this mode of current collection, and car 357 has the usual trolley-pole. These four-wheelers were restricted to rush-hour workings on the 10 route because of difficulties in crossing the sets of point wires designed for bow collector pick-up at John Watt Street and the Gate, Saltley. *T. J. Edgington*

The grey horse pulls the rather antiquated cart out of town along Prospect Row on 7 June 1950. This was a very prosperous area in Birmingham in the early years of the 19th century and led to the Vauxhall Gardens via Prospect Row and Ashted Row. By the mid-1850s, however, the great park had succumbed to the ever-increasing urban sprawl so that the whole area of Ashted had been built on within 20 years. EMB air-brake car 789 is about to squeeze past the horse and cart which is in front of the early-19th-century terraces that have obviously seen better days. *F. Lloyd*

The corner of Ashted Row and Great Francis Street marked the change from the older and originally prosperous early-19th-century area and the later mid-Victorian artisans' terraces that continued into neighbouring Saltley and Duddeston. Car 762, the first of the 1928 Brush-bodied EMB Burnley bogie air-brake cars, stands on the outward-bound curve of Ashted Row on its way to Alum Rock. The soldier who is striding purposefully across the road between the lorry and the rear of the tram is a reminder that the hostilities of the Second World War had not long been over and that National Service in the armed forces was in operation. *F. Lloyd Jones*

Car 769 is travelling towards the city centre on the 10 route and is turning into Ashted Row, having passed the Junction public house, owned by Atkinsons brewery who supplied their beer from the nearby Aston Park Brewery. Atkinsons were taken over by Mitchells & Butlers in 1959; the pub itself, however, fell victim, in 1950, to the largest redevelopment programme in the country which erased the previous street pattern and replaced it in 1952 with a group of brick-built 12-storey flats which have unofficially become known as 'The Dreadnoughts'. Just to the left of the pub is Bloomsbury Street, part of the route taken to Nechells by the horse trams which were abandoned in 1906. *F. Lloyd Jones*

The Victorian terraces of Great Francis Street and Saltley Road lacked everything except utilitarianism, and were to be demolished in the early 1950s as part of the Nechells Park Comprehensive Development area. They stood in the shadow of the ex-LNWR line to the North West, which opened as the Grand Junction Railway on 4 July 1837 and was the first line built in Birmingham. Behind the bridge are the gas holders at Saltley Gas Works.

Car 344 is having its pole turned after working the 62 route from Washwood Heath on 4 September 1950. Although the four-wheeler is in apparently good condition, it would be withdrawn on 30

September, to be broken up at Witton depot two months later. Beyond, bogie car 782 waits for the older tram to return to the out-of-city line. The rear of a passing prewar Daimler COG5 bus, probably working in from Glebe Farm, can be seen in Saltley Road. *T. J. Edgington*

Taken from virtually the same position as the photograph of 344 is this view taken in July 1992. Great Francis Street has disappeared and along with it all the original houses. Only the railway bridge, the two gas holders at Saltley Gas Works and the J. H. Richards factory have survived. *D. R. Harvey*

The same junction looking from Saltley Road towards the LNWR railway line and Saltley viaduct beyond on 29 October 1950. This scene had looked very much like this for many years, but it was to change the following day when the Washwood Heath-Alum Rock tram services would be converted to buses. The distant 'new look'-fronted Crossley DD42/7 bus is only a few months old and is working the 14 route from Glebe Farm. One of this class, 2489 (JOJ 489), has been preserved in full working order since 1969. The track in the foreground was the disconnected access for depot workings for the Nechells 7 route trams which had been the first BCT abandonment in 1922. The tracks remained, however, because of the necessity to use a skate return on the replacement trolleybus journeys from Bloomsbury Street to Washwood Heath depot. This lasted until the arcing from the skate on depot journeys resulted in the 'temporary' withdrawal of the route on 1 October 1940 - under the ARP lighting restrictions it was thought that the arcing would make the trolleybuses a target for Luftwaffe pilots, but it is debatable if this was true! *D. R. Harvey collection*

The little girl on her tricycle being shepherded by her father might have been envious of the young woman cyclist bouncing over the cobbles of Saltley Viaduct in the shadow of car 779 which has rumbled its way past Saltley railway station and is on its way to the Gate junction. This is just visible in the distance, where a Daimler COG5 on the Inner Circle 8 service is turning out of Adderley Road. To the left of the viaduct is the headquarters and works of Metropolitan-Cammell, where the body of the bus would have been constructed. *F. Lloyd Jones*

Looking in the opposite direction in late September 1950, the bus stop at Crawford Street on the east end of Saltley viaduct would soon be getting extra customers as the tram services were in their last week of operation. The notice of abandonment in the upper saloon balcony window of car 763 will mean that within days Birmingham would only have two groups of tram routes left, one on the high-speed track along Bristol Road and the other via Aston to serve the Erdington area. Car 763 is travelling in towards the city over Saltley viaduct with the gas holders towering over the industrial landscape. The aroma from the coal gas product plants was a noxious reminder of the main industry in the area. *R. T. Wilson*

The Gate at Saltley was where Washwood Heath Road swung to the left and Alum Rock Road went straight on. Car 770 was another of the large 62-seater Brush-bodied totally enclosed trams mounted on EMB Burnley maximum traction bogies of 1928. It is being used on the 62 route shortworking in Washwood Heath Road, and stands by a small row of shops adjacent to the junction. The main shops were round the corner from Barclays Bank in Alum Rock Road and survive today as the local Saltley shopping centre (see page 46). *R. T. Wilson*

The River Rea flows eastwards through Saltley in a wide and flat valley. In 1858 the first sewage filtration works was built on the Rea flood plain but with the population of Birmingham growing rapidly, by the 1860s the 140-acre plant was reduced to a 'sodden morass' with the most 'pestilent stench'. In 1884 the newly formed Tame and Rea District Drainage Board opened up a new sewage farm and the healthy state of the area was once more restored. The 1876 Building byelaws had prevented any further back-to-back housing developments, but by the late 1880s terraced through houses and tunnel-backs were being built, opening up the Washwood Heath area beyond the new sewage works, which had been common land until enclosure in 1817.

Car 798 passes the earliest of these Victorian developments at Havelock Road on its way along Washwood Heath Road to Ward End. The car is equipped with a trolley-pole, which had been fitted in the summer of 1950 when the car had been in Kyotts Lake Road Works in preparation for its use from Selly Oak depot. *R. T. Wilson*

BIRMINGHAM TRAMS 1933-53

Car 776, on the 10 route in Washwood Heath Road approaching the junction of Aston Church Road in 1949, is carrying the well-known Barbers Tea advertisement and is typical of the bow collector cars which spent all but 20 months of their 24-year service careers on the Washwood Heath depot routes. These cars were not generally as popular as the other air-brake cars, especially after they went to Selly Oak depot in 1950; their motormen disliked the uncertain air-braking system which was unique to the 50 cars of the 762 Class. *F. Lloyd Jones*

The inflexibility of the tramcar is shown here, as car 798 waits to pick up passengers in the middle of Washwood Heath Road outside Washwood Heath depot on 4 September 1950. A rather elderly Midland Red SOS REDD with an Eastern Counties H26/26R body, 1371 (HA 8016), speeds by. Built as late as 1932, it had three seats added to its upper saloon seating capacity and was withdrawn a few weeks later. With its antiquated frontal appearance, which rather reflected Midland Red's idiosyncratic views on vehicle design, it passes the somewhat 'beached' tram.

An equally peculiar feature of the later Birmingham tramcars was the desire that every passenger in the upper saloon should be able to regulate their own ventilation. This is the reason for the placing of eight windows between the bulkheads; from an aesthetic point of view, however, it did rather clutter up the traditionally graceful lines of Birmingham tramcars. *T. J. Edgington*

Strengthened Brush car 597 stands in Washwood Heath depot at about 4.00 pm on Sunday 23 July 1950 on an LRTL enthusiasts tour. It was on this day that the General Manager, Mr A. C. Baker, died at the age of 62.

The cars of the 587 Class were built in 1920 and were the last cars to be delivered with open balconies, which were enclosed on all the class between 1927 and 1931. The steel strengthening plates across the lower saloon bulkhead window were fitted to nine of the class. These 50 trams, mounted on Brush maximum traction Burnley bogies, reached a maximum mileage in their 33 years of service of some 969,500 miles. The class provided the citizens of Birmingham with their last tramcar, 616, as well as this tram, 597, which had the dubious distinction of being the last passenger tramcar to be dismantled at Kyotts Lake Road Works on 6 August 1953. *S. N. J. White*

BIRMINGHAM TRAMS 1933-53

Left One of the last 26 open-balconied four-wheel trams in service was car 381. It was transferred from Miller Street to Washwood Heath depot on 10 September 1949 and ran until the day before the Washwood Heath closure. These 301 Class cars were built to a height of 15 ft 7 1/2 in which enabled them to have a universal route availability and to some extent made them the most useful cars on the system. It is standing with car 768 in Washwood Heath Road just below the depot entrance and near the Leigh Road junction. This led to the Midland Railway Carriage & Wagon Company (MRCW) factory which eventually became the Metropolitan-Cammell bus-building works, which finally closed in late 1989. *R. T. Wilson*

Below left As Birmingham spread out into the countryside in the late 19th century, so the need for public recreational open space became more important. In 1903 the city purchased some 53 acres of land in Ward End, which included the rather splendid Georgian home of Birmingham's first historian, William Hutton, who, in 1781, had written *The History of Birmingham*. A large ornamental boating pool, fed by a natural spring, was built in 1909, while an aviary and a winter garden were added just prior to the First World War. This open space became Ward End Park, on whose wall on the right two prospective Midland Red passengers are waiting. Opposite them people are queuing to alight from and get on to car 773. The stop here at Drews Lane had become one of the busiest in the city as it catered for the workforce of the Wolseley Motors factory which, by 1950, had become Morris Motors Ltd. *R. T. Wilson*

Above right Washwood Heath Road rises steadily uphill after Ward End Park and passes through an area of pre-First World War housing and the Ward End shopping area. Car 767, having just been passed by a Ford Anglia, has reached Bamville Road at the bottom of the row of shops. *F. Lloyd Jones*

Below The final approach to the Washwood Heath terminus at the Fox and Goose public house was on a 600-yard stretch of reserved track from Chetwynd Road along the north side of Washwood Heath Road. The houses on the side of the reservation date from the mid-1920s, while those on the right in this view just predate the First World War. Fischer bow collector-equipped 769 has just left the street track and crossed the road to enter the reserved track. Noticeable in this view, silhouetted against the sky, is the shaped piece of wood fitted to the edge of the roof of the tram in place of the metal roof guttering; apparently, when new the bow collector fixing brackets could make the guttering become live. This car was modified at Washwood Heath in October 1928 to eliminate this problem, but cars 774-811 were modified by the Brush Company before delivery. In the background is open balcony 301 Class car 357 which, unlike 769, is carrying the simpler postwar style of number. *W. A. Camwell*

Above The short length of reserved track between Chetwynd Road and the Fox and Goose terminus served as a useful parking place for trams when Washwood Heath depot was being converted into a bus garage in the summer of 1950. At evenings and weekends cars were stabled on both tracks and the service curtailed at a temporary crossover a short distance from the terminus. Cars 801 and 806 head the lines of parked cars some weeks before the final abandonment. The reserved track was built in anticipation of a dual carriageway scheme which had to wait until the late 1970s before it came to fruition. *L. Mason*

Below The reserved track finally became a dual carriageway some 25 years after the last tram used it. The shops on the right on the corner of Alum Rock Road, which date from the 1930s, still remain, but other than the Fox and Goose public house everything else in the earlier photograph has been altered, though tantalisingly it is all still recognisable. MCW 'Metrobus' Mk II 2388 (LOA 388X) is on the 93 route from Chelmsley Wood Estate in July 1992. *D. R. Harvey*

Right At 1.40 pm on 2 September 1950 two buses pass each other on the Outer Circle route. The one loading passengers in Bromford Lane on the extreme left is an FOF-registered Daimler COG5 of 1939 on a shortworking to Perry Barr. The 1947 Daimler CVA6 on the right negotiates the island on its clockwise journey around the 11 bus route. The sign of the Fox and Goose public house can be seen behind car 776. These Brush-built cars were fitted with EMB Burnley bogies and were the only cars in the BCT fleet to be equipped with the EMB air wheel and track brake system. They ran with powerful Dick, Kerr DK30/1L 63 hp motors. Washwood Heath drivers quite often exploited the speed potential of these cars and their bow collector current collection with some spirited running. By this time car 776 had been equipped with a trolley-pole prior to being sent to Selly Oak to work the Bristol Road routes just one month later. *A. N. H. Glover*

BIRMINGHAM TRAMS 1933-53

Above The magnificent mock-Tudor Beaufort Cinema at the Washwood Heath terminus was opened on 4 August 1929 and was fitted with a two-manual, eight-unit Compton organ. This instrument was played by Reginald New who, in the 1930s, did radio broadcasts for the BBC from the Beaufort. The instrument was eventually removed to the EMI studio at St John's Wood, London, in 1937, and the cinema itself was finally closed on 19 August 1978. Car 787, seen on 17 July 1949, is unusually carrying an advertisement for E. R. Green, who were based in High Street, Kings Heath, and were well known as a ladies' clothier. The Beaufort is showing the film 'The Street with No Name' starring Mark Stevens, an American leading man who usually appeared in routine B movies. Also appearing in this film, made in 1948, was Richard Widmark; it was his third major film before he moved on to star in films such as 'The Alamo' and 'Madigan'. *O. M. Capes*

Alum Rock

THE Alum Rock 8 route was opened on 1 January 1907 and was worked by the newly opened Washwood Heath depot. It left from the second barrier from the top of Martineau Street and followed the Washwood Heath route as far as the Gate, whence it climbed Alum Rock Road through the busy Saltley shopping centre as far as Highfield Road. It was extended from here to Belchers Lane terminus at the Pelham on 14 October 1925 to serve the newly built council houses in the Cotterills Lane area. This was the last major section of new street tramway to be built in the city.

The details of the operation of the Alum Rock Road route were the same as the Washwood Heath route and it was abandoned on the same Saturday night.

Left Although the Alum Rock route went straight on at the Gate, Saltley, the 8 service always seemed to be on the less important road. After leaving the Atkinsons-owned, late-19th-century Gate public house, the trams entered the shopping centre which went to the top of the hill where the original 1907 terminus at Highfield Road was reached. On 16th August 1950 passengers are boarding car 789 which will shortly negotiate the junction with Washwood Heath Road. This area, except for the pub and a few of the shops, has barely changed over the intervening years. *R. T. Wilson*

Below left The thriving shopping centre in Alum Rock Road, seen on the same day, 16 August 1950, looking down towards the Gate junction, was very close to Saltley Gas Works, which can be seen in the background. The driver of the early postwar Austin 8 car seems unsure as to whether to pass on the inside of tram 795, which has apparently just left the stop next to the car. It will leave Saltley's bustling Victorian shopping district for the grimy industrial landscape of the River Rea valley as it crosses Saltley viaduct. *R. T. Wilson*

Above The Rock cinema in Alum Rock Road can be seen above the surrounding shops beyond the tram in this 17 September 1950 view. It was opened on 15 January 1934, and compared to the shops, such as the Maypole Dairy Co Ltd and The Gate Fish and Chip Saloon, it seemed the height of luxury, although the opening bill, part of which was a Laurel and Hardy short, was, perhaps, not quite what the customers expected on such an auspicious occasion. The cinema closed in 1972, the Maypole Dairy Co ceased trading many years ago and the chip shop has been replaced by much more exotic Balti-type fare.

   Car 770 waits to pick up passengers on the 8 route. It carries an advertisement for the *Birmingham Gazette*, a newspaper which only survived the trams by three years after 215 years of publication. *J. E. Gready*

Below The original terminus in Alum Rock Road was here at the top of the hill at Highfield Road; car 102 is seen leaving in the direction of the distant Saltley gas holders and the city centre in about 1914. It is in almost original condition with open vestibules and flop-over destination boards. Although only 30 years old, the shops have about them the well-worn look of an area which is past its first flush of youth. Yet it is a suburb which survives today, looking very much the same as it did in that long, hot summer before all innocence was lost. *Commercial postcard, D. R. Harvey collection*

Above Car 762 is photographed in Alum Rock Road on 4 September 1950 with only about a month left before the route was abandoned. It is travelling towards the city and is about half a mile from the old terminus at Highfield Road. Jephcott Road, which the tram is passing, marked a transition point in the growth of the city along this route. To the left, behind the trees, are the last Victorian/early-20th-century shops, while opposite them are some of the earliest post-First World War council houses in Birmingham. They were built in Cotterills Lane and were first occupied in 1919. This area looks very much the same today except for the now far more mature trees. *R. T. Wilson*

Below A Morrison BM-type battery-electric bread van stands at the junction of Cotterills Lane and Alum Rock Road as car 803 swings round from the nearby terminus at Belchers Lane. The one-mile extension of the route to the Pelham Arms pub was opened on 14 October 1925, and was the last piece of street tramway opened in Birmingham; the six subsequent tramway extensions were built along reserved track and were therefore designed for faster running. The Alum Rock service catered for the municipal housing estate. *R. T. Wilson*

Car 789 stands in the terminal stub of the terminus on 4 June 1950 with the Pelham Arms in the background, an imposing council estate public house built in the mid-1920s by Mitchells & Butlers. Car 789 clearly shows the advantages on a warm day of eight upper saloon windows, as every row of seats had access to an opening window. The car is in its final 1948-style livery, with advertisements for Bovril and the new Dreft washing powder; many Birmingham trams by this time could be identified from the combination of advertisements which they carried. This 1950 view recalls the lack of vehicular traffic at the time - there is no other vehicle in sight! *T. J. Edgington*

The cluster of shops at Belchers Lane at the terminus of the 8 tram route, looking in the opposite direction on 4 September 1950. The conductor of car 768 is about to help the little girl onto the platform of the tram, while beyond it car 773 is waiting for 768 to depart for the city before itself entering the terminal stub. The shops are typical of the small retailers which developed in the suburbs. A butcher, tobacconist and greengrocer are to the right, while beyond the small lorry is a Timothy Whites & Taylors chemist. Next door but one is Pearks Dairies Ltd, grocers and provisioners, whose shop probably gave off that wonderful smell of smoked bacon so characteristic of such shops before the advent of the supermarket. *R. T. Wilson*

Left The full splendour of the Birmingham tramcar can really only be appreciated in the prewar livery as shown here by tramcar 637. Miller Street depot operated the complete batch of two classes of trams numbered from 637 to 701 in the years immediately before the outbreak of the Second World War. Car 637, the first of the MRCW cars, is seen working the 6 route to Perry Barr in Corporation Street in September 1938. It is passing through a section of Birmingham's notorious one way street system and is running against the flow of other vehicular traffic as it crosses the entrance to the Old Square on the left. A Midland Red SOS FEDD can just be seen behind it coming into the city. *Colour-Rail*

Above One of Washwood Heath depot's 762-811 Class of Brush-bodied EMB air-brake cars stands at the unloading stop in Dale End after working into the city from Alum Rock on the 8 route. Car 803, with a pram firmly wedged on the platform, awaits the signal to move off and turn right into Martineau Street where it will reload for the 2½-mile journey back to the Pelham. Car 803 led a fairly quiet life, running from 1928 until 1950 from Washwood Heath depot and then from 5 October 1950 until July 1952 at Selly Oak. It was broken up at Witton in August 1952. This late 1950 view shows it with the notices in the balcony windows informing the public of the abandonment of the Washwood Heath routes in October 1950. *C. Carter*

The Erdington terminus was within yards of the city boundary with Sutton Coldfield and was just beyond the Yenton public house and the main Chester Road. The terminal stub was a short section of side reservation amid the thriving suburban shopping centre. Car 730, an all-electric GEC-motored Brush-built tram of 1925, stands waiting to return to the city, as a grey two-door Morris Minor speeds past along Sutton Road. It is getting fairly near to the end of the BCT tram system, and the side panels reveal at least four partly torn advertisements, giving a run-down appearance to the tram. Only a few years earlier this would not have been tolerated, but somehow such a trivial detail seemed to matter less when 'the dinosaurs were doomed'. *Leeds Transport Historical Society*

MRCW car 647 coasts into the tram stop island at Salford Bridge, Gravelly Hill, to meet slightly older Brush-built car 632 of 1920. The latter is loading up with passengers before it continues its journey into the city. Both trams are working on the 79 route to Pype Hayes Park and 647 will turn right in front of the public toilets and travel along Tyburn Road to the terminus some two miles away. The date is late June 1953 and the trams have only a few days left in service before the final closing ceremony. *W. J. Wyse*

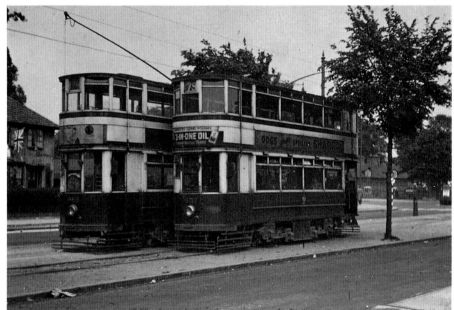

Coronation flags still adorn one of the 1920s council houses in this June 1953 view of Pype Hayes terminus. Cars 632 and 688 stand beside each other a few yards from the single-line terminal stub that led to the passenger shelters. Both cars have the boarded-over staircase window which was applied fairly arbitrarily to the postwar fleet. Behind the trams, beyond the traffic island, is Pype Hayes Park which, with its golf course, straddled the Birmingham-Sutton Coldfield boundary. *W. J. Wyse*

The last of the 1920 Brush-built trams, 636, speeds along the central reservation in Streetly Road in late June 1953. It has just left the terminus at the top of the hill and is passing the Stockland Green recreation ground in the bottom of the valley between the terminus and Stockland Green. This section of central reservation was opened on 23 June 1926 and was one of the last four route extensions built on the Birmingham system, the others being on Tyburn Road, Hall Green and Bordesley Green. When the extension was first opened from Stockland Green the demand for trams to the new terminus was so low that trams alternated between Stockland Green and Short Heath. *W. J. Wyse*

PERRY BARR, WITTON AND LOZELLS

Perry Barr

THIS route was opened from Martineau Street to Newtown Row on 1 January 1907, and was extended to Chain Walk, which is just beyond Six Ways, Aston, on 23 April 1907. Unfortunately, because of problems with interworking, the through service to Perry Barr was not opened until 8 December 1909.

Starting from the top stand in Martineau Street, the 6 route followed the Washwood Heath cars along Corporation Street but carried on past the Victoria Law Courts to Corporation Place. Here it crossed through the complicated traffic island arrangement and turned into Lancaster Street which was lined with warehouses and factories. On reaching Princip Street, the route climbed over

the steep rise of the Birmingham & Fazeley canal bridge, whose crest was marked by an ornate wrought iron urinal.

Beyond here lay Newtown Row, with its linear shopping centre that extended as far as the Bartons Arms. On either side lay a tightly packed area of mid-19th-century housing. Immediately behind Newtown Row and parallel to it on the western side was Summer Lane. This road, through apocryphal and true stories about it, perhaps epitomised the real hard-working, hard-playing Brummie of the first half of this century.

On leaving the shops, public houses and the music hall in Newtown Row, the 6 service climbed up to High Street through another shopping centre to reach Six Ways, Aston. Here the 3 route turned right into Witton Road, while the Perry Barr route continued past Chain Walk,

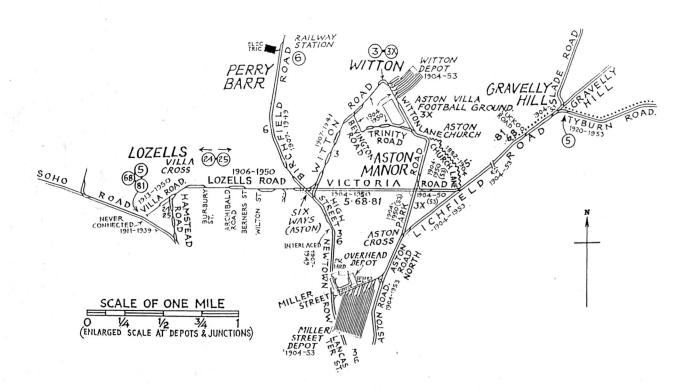

Perry Barr, Witton and Lozells routes

where, for eighteen months, a tram was parked every day to act as a waiting room for passengers travelling between the Chain Walk shuttle and the main service from Birmingham.

Birchfield Road gradually opened out into a tree-lined road with large Victorian villas in their own capacious grounds. The route crossed Aston Lane at the Birchfield Road shopping centre. Here was Perry Barr depot which had been taken over from Handsworth UDC and was intermittently a running depot for the Perry Barr service. The tram route terminated just short of Perry Barr station almost outside the New Crown & Cushion public house.

The 6 route was, for most of their careers, the preserve of the trams of the 1-20 Class, although the two ex-CBT bogie cars, 451 and 452, were latterly to be found on it. Other newer totally enclosed trams were found on the route in later years.

The route was abandoned on 31 December 1949.

The 6 route to Perry Barr started at a kerbside loading barrier at the top of Martineau Street outside Preedy's tobacconist shop. In this 1949 view the passengers are boarding car 13, one of only six of the 1-20 Class which survived the Second World War. They were originally built by the Electric Railway & Tramway Carriage Works Ltd (ER&TCW) in 1904 as 56-seater open-top reversed-staircase double-deckers, but cars 11-20 were quickly rebuilt with top covers by UEC which gave the cars an overall height of 16 ft 3 in. As this was some 9 inches higher than later top-covered cars, these Miller Street-allocated trams were used almost exclusively on the 6 route, which had no height restrictions on it.

The tram, once loaded, will swing into Corporation Street in front of the Cobden Hotel. The Dolcis shoe shop, in the years just after the war, had one of the potentially dangerous self-X-ray machines for viewing your own feet! *R. T. Wilson*

The rather splendid late-1920s Austin crosses the tramlines from Martineau Street just after car 15 turns down Corporation Street on the 6 route. The tram will cross Bull Street before reaching the white concrete expanse of the distant Lewis's store on the left.

This was as near to the heart of Birmingham as trams ever reached. With no cross-city workings, the tram routes often had their own specific car types peculiar to that route; if the Lodge Road had the Brill-Maleys, then the 6 route had the open-balconied bogie cars. Sometimes known as the 'Old Bogies', they gave splendid service to the city. This view, taken in about 1932, shows car 15 with the gold lining-out on the dash panel that was so characteristic of the prewar livery. This car was bomb damaged in January 1941, then stored until broken up in 1946. *R. T. Wilson*

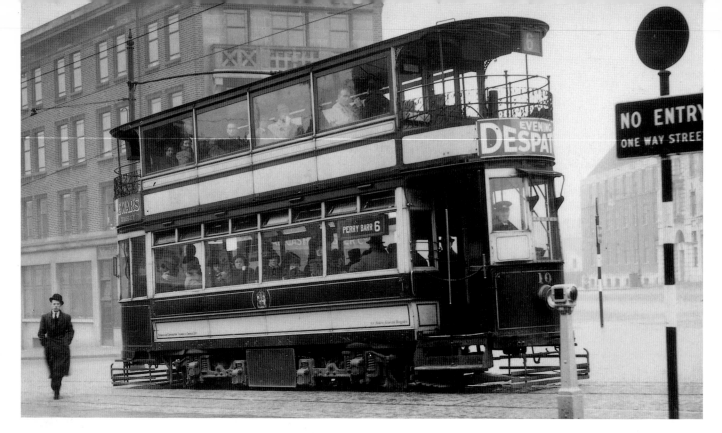

Corporation Place is now a three-level road junction, but when car 10 was crossing it on 18 March 1939 the two main features were, on the extreme right, the Central Fire Station, opened in 1935, and Halfords Cycle Co Ltd. The latter building was destroyed by fire on 12 March 1955, much to the embarrassment of the fire service. Car 10 was top-covered by G. C. Milnes, Voss & Co Ltd, in March 1905, and subsequently fitted with upholstered transverse seats, EMB Burnley bogies and 40 hp motors. This conversion work increased the weight by some 2¹/₂ tons, which meant that the car's performance was not particularly sparkling. Car 10 was one of 24 trams destroyed on the night of 9-10 April 1941 when Miller Street was hit in an air-raid by an oil bomb. *A. N. H. Glover*

Cars returning to the city via Corporation Place turned across the front of the Central Fire Station into Stafford Street, whose one-way single line took the inbound trams to Dale End. At the outer end factories like Harris & Sheldon Ltd dominated the scene. Car 570 was one of 75 UEC-bodied 62-seater trams which were mounted on Mountain & Gibson Burnley maximum traction bogies. It had been transferred to Miller Street depot after the Stratford Road abandonments of January 1937 and remained there until the BCT system closed in 1953. *R. T. Wilson*

At the far end of Stafford Street the splendid industrial buildings gave way to a series of rather time-worn three-storied terraces, most of which had been converted into small individual shops. The Corner Cafe seen here on the right, with its pseudo-Greek portico, looked out over the junction with Coleshill Street to the right, and to John Watt Street to the left, which was used by the Washwood Heath routes. By the mid-1950s the cafe had become the Shah Jahan, one of the first Indian restaurants in Birmingham. Car 686, a Brush-car built in December 1924, trundles towards this junction before running up to Dale End and the Martineau Street terminus. *F. Lloyd Jones*

Car 656, on the 6 route, and 811, numerically the last of the EMB air-brake cars, on the 10 route, stand in Dale End on 27 December 1949. Dale End was one of the oldest streets in Birmingham, although precious little of it remains today. It was originally the main road to Lichfield and, as such in the 18th and 19th centuries became a street of commerce and industry. John Taylor set up his japanning works, which employed over 500 people, in Crooked Lane off Dale End. In 1765 Taylor and Sampson Lloyd II set up Taylor and Lloyd's bank, which was later to become Lloyds Bank, one of the 'big four' national banks. *T. J. Edgington*

Looking again at the outward-going 6 service, the trams turned from Corporation Place into Lancaster Street which would take the tram route to Newtown Row. The warehouses and factories in this wide, cobbled thoroughfare, such as Stanley Croft and Brown, Hopwood and Gilbert, tower over car 452 as it passes Lench Street. Cars 451 and 452 were, at 34 ft 8 in, the two longest cars in the Birmingham fleet, these stately trams being known locally as 'The Titanics'. They were fitted with Dick, Kerr DK13A 40 hp motors and travelled sedately about their business until the last day of 1949 when the Perry Barr route was abandoned. Built as car 180 for the City of Birmingham Tramways Co (CBT), 452 was originally an open-topper and subsequently, during the First World War, a single-decker used in trailer experiments on the Washwood Heath route. *D. Griffiths*

The other ex-CBT bogie car 'twin' was 451, which had been 178 in the original owner's fleet and which is seen here negotiating the steep Birmingham & Fazeley canal bridge. The motorcyclist overtaking on the blind humpback bridge must have worked out the odds against another tramcar rearing up in front of him. It is December 1949 and car 451 is nearing the end of 46 years of service during which it ran some 650,000 miles. It was fitted with a CBT-built, 68-seater, five-bay-construction body, which further emphasised the length of the tram.

Car 451 is quite near the premises of William Shillock, a boot and shoe manufacturer, of 73 Newtown Row, from whose shop window on Thursday 12 September 1895 the original FA Cup was stolen. It had been on display after Aston Villa had won it, beating West Bromwich Albion 1-0. *R. T. Wilson*

There was an offer by BCT to sell car 452 for preservation, but nothing occurred. This was a great pity as the asking price was reputedly below £50. It was retained for a few months, but broken up in April 1950.

Car 452 is seen in Newtown Row passing Cowper Street on its outward journey to Perry Barr on 22 November 1949. This area of Aston had started to develop in 1835 and was given the name of Newtown to distinguish it from the original Aston village about a mile away to the northeast. The area, although run down, always had the feel of a busy, lively, tight-knit community, with its shops, theatre and picture house. Yet all was swept away in the rebuilding of Newtown; designed to remove the notorious Summer Lane area, it only succeeded in replacing it with an environment of shopping precincts and multistorey flats, which in the end, of course, no one wanted. *T. J. Edgington*

Car 3 stands in Newtown Row with a lazy destination number box which had probably been turned by children riding on the balcony. It is working the 6 route and has reached St Stephen's church, built in the Early English style in brick and sandstone and consecrated in 1844. It finally closed its doors in 1950, just a few months after the final abandonment of the Perry Barr trams. Car 3, by this time something of a venerable vehicle, seems to have a lower saloon that is at odds with the much more perpendicular upper saloon. Newtown Row continued towards the Aston Hippodrome, which is just discernible beyond the 1-20 Class tram in the far distance. *F. Lloyd Jones*

The half-price footwear for sale at N. B. Shoes, on the corner of Inkerman Street and High Street, Newtown, Aston, appears to be creating some interest as groups of people do their shopping one Saturday morning in November 1949. Car 581 has just turned on to the short section of interlaced track in front of 'The House That Jack Built' store, which was just beyond the shoppers to the right. The tram is just above the culverted Hockley Brook, a tributary stream of the River Rea, which in medieval times had been a problem to cross.

Tram 581 entered service in February 1914 and, together with 582-4, was used in the short-lived 'first class' experiment along the recently opened Hagley Road route. Its dashes were painted yellow, the lower saloon seats were covered in blue plush cushions and rubber matting was laid on the floor. Brown curtains were fitted and notices proclaiming 'First Class Car' and 'Double Fares' were displayed. *F. Lloyd Jones*

Passengers board car 677 in High Street, Newtown, in 1949. This was one of 40 trams ordered in 1924 from the Brush Electrical Company of Loughborough, who supplied the 63-seater bodies. It was mounted on EMB maximum traction bogies and fitted with English Electric 40 hp motors; 33 ft 6 in long and weighing some 16 tons, it spent all its 29-year service life working from Miller Street depot. It stands opposite the Bartons Arms, and just visible behind the tram is the Globe Cinema (formerly the Globe Electric Palace) which was opened in August 1913 and closed in September 1955; the entrance, on the corner of New Street and High Street, was surmounted by a dome or globe-like structure. Car 677 will ascend High Street while car 570, a tram some ten years older, makes its way towards the city. *F. Lloyd Jones*

Car 657, one of the 1923 MRCW 637-661 Class, is seen travelling towards the city on the cobbled High Street hill. The tall gabled building is the impressive Bartons Arms public house; opened in 1901, this Grade II listed building, one of the most famous pubs in Birmingham, is noted for its tile painted walls, stained glass windows and wooden snob-screens in the smoke rooms. *R. T. Wilson*

The distant clock stands on the Midland Bank's premises at the corner of Lozells Road and Birchfield Road at Six Ways, Aston, and marks one of the most complicated sections of trackwork in Birmingham, with five of the six roads carrying tramlines. The 5 route, Birmingham's only inter-urban service, from Lozells to Gravelly Hill, crossed High Street, Six Ways, Aston, where car 583 is standing, and went into Victoria Road, which is on the distant right behind the Morris 10 saloon. The steep hill of Witton Road took the 3 route towards Witton depot and Villa Park, a service withdrawn in early September 1939. Only Alma Street, which carried the 33 Kingstanding bus route and ran behind the buildings on the left, did not carry a tram route.

In this 1949 view, the tram is passing a Morrison Electricar DV 4-type battery electric dustcart. This one, No 221 (FVP 85), was built in 1940 and had a working career of nearly 25 years. Birmingham had the largest fleet of battery electric dustcarts in the country, and between 1918 and 1971 operated 262 vehicles. *R. T. Wilson*

Car 20, one of the six postwar survivors of the 1-20 Class, stands in Birchfield Road, Six Ways, on the 6 route on Tuesday 22 November 1949. It is in the 1946 simplified postwar livery, with the prewar fleet number style. This car had been top-covered by UEC in July 1907; this could easily be identified because the entrance door to the upper saloon had a flat top which followed the roof profile, rather than the earlier arched entrance door and roofs of the G. C. Milnes, Voss-built top-covers. The tram had its original Brill 22E maximum traction bogies replaced with Brush Burnley-type bogies, and DK13A 40 hp motors were also fitted in about 1924. Car 20 continued in this condition until the closure of the Perry Barr route on 31 December 1949.
T. J. Edgington

On leaving Six Ways the Perry Barr route reached Chain Walk. For nearly two years, from 1907, this was the terminus - through working to Perry Barr was prohibited because of a dispute with Handsworth UDC. Passengers had to change from one Corporation car to another; as a result of this difficulty, it was the practice to take a spare tram from Birchfield Road depot each morning and park it at Chain Walk to serve as a waiting room for transferring passengers. Here car 579 leaves the short section of single line track at Mansfield Road on its inward-bound journey. *F. Lloyd Jones*

The Perry Barr shopping centre had developed on either side of the Aston Lane junction. There was a small row of early-20th-century shops in Birchfield Road dominated by the Birchfield cinema, opened in 1913, which is being passed in this rare 1946 view by car 345 working the 6 route. The tram is still painted in the wartime grey livery which it retained until withdrawal in August 1947. Car 20, in front of it, has the prewar livery with cream-painted rocker panels. To the left is Birchfield Road garage, which had been taken over from Handsworth UDC in 1911. The two BCT buses in the distance are a Daimler COG5, still with khaki-painted roof and rear dome, and an MOS Brush-rebodied AEC 'Regent', 397 (OG 397), of 1930 vintage. A BMMO FEDD, one of only three to be built as a full-front vehicle, can also be seen, still in its prewar livery. *V. E. Burrows*

On a gloomy Wednesday 28 December 1949 car 18 stands at the New Crown & Cushion terminus near to Perry Barr railway station, with posters in its window announcing the imminent abandonment of the tram service just three days later. Perry Barr was the city boundary until 1928 and by that date the days of tramway extensions were over. In fact, the 33 bus route to Kingstanding was opened in 1929 and this effectively ended any chance of extending the 6 route. The terminus of the route, served faithfully by the 1-20 Class, therefore remained at Perry Barr for some 40 years. Note the Foden BRS lorry crossing the railway bridge. *A. N. H. Glover*

BIRMINGHAM TRAMS 1933-53

Witton routes

THE 3 route left Six Ways, Aston, and descended the steep hill in Witton Road past the former Aston Council House and going through sections of double and single line before arriving at Witton Square where it met the 3X route. The 3 route had been opened by CBT in 1904 and was taken over on 1 January 1912. It was the only branch off the main 6 route and was part of a circular service with the 3X route around Witton; however, the 3 route was suspended for the duration of the Second World War after 9 September 1939 and was not restored at the end of the hostilities, although the line remained intact until 1947.

The 3X route followed the Aston Road routes as far as Aston Cross where it climbed up Park Road between Ansells brewery and the nearby HP Sauce factory in Tower Street. It crossed the junction with Victoria Road before passing Aston Hall on a 1 in 20 descent to turn left in front of the splendid Aston parish church. This hill caused two car-wrecking accidents with 323 in 1932 and 714 in 1940 succumbing to brake failure and driver error.

The 3X route then passed Villa Park, opposite a line of very distinctive pre-First World War semi-detached houses across the road from the ground, before reaching the terminus at the Witton Arms public house opposite the former CBT depot. The car would then continue back to the city via Witton Road and Six Ways, Aston.

Always in BCT days associated with the 301 Class, the 3X route, which had survived in a truncated form, lasted until it was replaced by the 39 bus, the last trams running on 31 December 1949. The depot remained in use until 1953, and as a result the line remained intact until the closure of the system.

The main Lichfield Road routes can be seen in the distance, with a tram on the 79 service standing at Aston Cross in front of Ansells brewery. Alongside the brewery ran Park Road, the scene of this photograph; the majority of this link between Aston Cross and Witton was swept away when the Aston Expressway was opened in May 1972.

Park Road was part of the 3X tram route to Witton depot and also for football specials to Villa Park. Car 691, on a Villa Park football special, has just passed a horse and cart, appropriately carrying wooden beer barrels, and is climbing past the rather shabby shops opposite the brewery. It is late 1949 and Hollings Cafe, with a few pieces of decorative tinsel in the window, is offering the bargain of five mince pies for a shilling. *R. T. Wilson*

Once at the top of Park Road the 3X route crossed the inter-urban 5 service at Victoria Road and descended the steep hill towards Aston parish church, with its graceful 15th-century tower. Park Road itself was a strange contrast. Beyond the Wolverhampton-registered Hillman Minx lay Aston Hall and its surrounding park; built by the Holte family between 1618 and 1635, it is one of the finest Jacobean houses in the country. Yet on this grey Wednesday, 28 December 1949, car 631 climbs past the Sycamore public house and the Victorian terraces which look even more uninviting than normal. *A. N. H. Glover*

Car 537, one of the former open-balconied UEC bogie cars, is seen at Aston parish church in 1949. This tram had previously been at Rosebery Street depot, but after the closure of the Ladywood route it was transferred to Witton depot where it stayed until early 1950. It is standing approximately where car 714 overturned in March 1940, injuring some 30 passengers. This wartime accident was caused when the tram failed to make the turn into Witton Lane at Park Road when the driver lost control; the roof and the upper deck broke apart. In the resultant enquiry the driver was blamed for failing to make the compulsory stop on Park Lane hill. *R. T. Wilson*

Crowds of Aston Villa supporters walk past the Holte public house in Trinity Road on Tuesday 27 December 1949 for the

return match from the previous day with Wolverhampton Wanderers. Unfortunately, the largest crowd of the season at Villa Park, no fewer than 69,492, saw the Villa lose 4-1! UEC car 356 is the only open-balconied four-wheeler in this view and it is still in prewar livery; the gold lining-out on the dash panel and the cream-painted rocker panel distinguish this style from that introduced in 1946.

The trams often had to cater for crowds of over 40,000, all three Birmingham area football grounds, Villa Park, St Andrews (Birmingham City), and The Hawthorns (West Bromwich Albion), being served by tramcar routes. Villa Park was the last to be served by trams, the route being abandoned on 31 December 1949. *T. J. Edgington*

A few days later, on New Year's Eve 1949, Aston Villa had a home fixture against Newcastle United, and 39,803 fans turned out for the game. Once again Villa supporters went home to their end of year festivities with heavy hearts as the home team was beaten 1-0, giving Newcastle the double over the home side.

Also that night the Witton and Perry Barr routes were abandoned, and later that evening car 373, in full postwar livery, was temporarily parked with other trams which were due for scrapping, with lights ablaze, in Trinity Road next to Aston Park. This was done so that more room could be made for cars running into Witton depot for the last time. Car 373 went into store the same evening and was broken up in March 1950. *F. Lloyd Jones*

Witton Square, at the end of Witton Lane, marked the terminus of the 3X route. As mentioned above, until the outbreak of the Second World War it had been a circular route; the 3 service, which came down Witton Road from Six Ways, Aston, also terminated at Witton Square, and its track can be seen turning to the left in front of the butcher's shop beyond the waiting tram. These lines were subsequently only used for football specials.

Car 610, one of the 1920 cars with Brush bodies, open balconies and Brush Burnley maximum traction bogies, stands at the Aston Hotel on 17 July 1949, between the entrance tracks to Witton depot and next to the Bundy clock. This car suffered severe accident damage in February 1950 and was broken up the following month. *C. C. Thornburn*

As a result of the closure of the Lozells and Washwood Heath routes at the end of September 1950, surplus trams were broken up at Witton depot. By this time it was not needed for operational purposes and was used variously for storing buses and scrapping redundant tramcars until November 1952 when it became a running shed until the final closure. It is October 1950 and Car 552 stands at the front of a line of trams earmarked for scrapping. On the left is works car PW8, a former CBT double-decker that had been transferred the same month to manoeuvre trams around as they were being dismantled. The remains of a lower saloon can be seen against the wall on the right. This desolate scene would be repeated both here and at Kyotts Lake Road Works until after the final abandonment. Happily, the depot is now the Aston Manor Transport Museum and contains many interesting vehicles mainly from the West Midlands area. *R. T. Wilson*

Witton Square lay just a few yards beyond Witton depot and it was here that cars 320 and 331 were posed for photographs on the curve into Witton Road; car 320 has had its destination blind turned round to show the withdrawn 3 route. Both cars are in basically prewar livery. This 301 Class of UEC-built four-wheel cars displays the typical characteristics of Birmingham tramcar design: they have hexagonal dash panels and the handbrake cowling which produced the distinctive small vestibule window. Also visible on 320 is the balcony wing window designed to protect passengers from the elements on the open part of the staircase. The presence of the early postwar Metro-Cammell-bodied Daimler CVA6 bus in the background suggests that this is a view taken in 1949. *W. A. Camwell*

Standing in Bevington Road at the end of a row of eight Villa Park Football Special trams in 1949 is car 777, parked in this side street during the football match at Villa Park. This tram, in common with all the 762 Class cars from Washwood Heath depot, was fitted with a Fischer bow collector. Until that depot's closure for trams in October 1950, the Villa Park excursions were virtually these trams' only sojourn away from the 8 and 10 routes. Car 777 later became the tram that closed the Bristol Road routes at about midnight on 5 July 1952.

Darlington's ironmongers, with its galvanised buckets, pans and sundry items of domestic drudgery, is obviously finding the competition of the many thousand football fans at Villa Park a little too much - trade seems a little slow in Bevington Road on this November day. *R. T. Wilson*

BIRMINGHAM TRAMS 1933-53

Lozells

THE Lozells route was Birmingham's only real inter-suburban tram service. Opened between Lozells and Gravelly Hill by CBT on 7 May 1906, it was taken over by BCT on 1 January 1912 and was abandoned on 30 September 1950. It was always operated by Witton depot and in BCT days used 301 Class four-wheelers and 512 Class bogie cars.

The route started from Villa Cross but was extended by BCT to Villa Road on 8 January 1913 within a few yards of the main Soho Road trams, although there was never any physical connection.

On leaving the terminus, the 5 route went past some of the large Victorian villas that typified residential Handsworth, before arriving at the Hamstead Road junction where the 24 and 25 routes turned into Villa Road. The shopping centre here was known as 'the village' and was for many years one of the better-known suburban shopping centres in Birmingham.

After passing Villa Cross, the cinema with the large ornate rose window above the entrance and the Villa Cross public house in the angle between Lozells Road and Heathfield Road, the trams used sections of double and single track through the mixed Victorian residential and shopping area to Six Ways, Aston, which, as has already been mentioned, was one of the most complicated track layouts on the BCT system. Crossing the junction, the route then went along Victoria Road and intersected the 3X route at Park Road. As the Victoria Road descended to join Lichfield Road, so the size and quality of the houses deteriorated.

The route turned left onto Lichfield Road and followed the Aston Road routes to Gravelly Hill. Here at the tram terminus the cars unloaded at the shelters before turning into Tyburn Road and then reversing on the central reservation before returning to the shelters to load up. At peak times the route was extended along Tyburn Road to Fort Dunlop as a 63 route. It was also extended to Erdington as a 68 tram on Sundays until 1923, and to Pype Hayes as an 81 on summer Sundays from 1928 to 1930.

The western terminus of the Lozells route was in Villa Road, but although it was just a few yards away from the tracks in Soho Road that carried the routes to Handsworth and West Bromwich, a connecting line was never built. It is 7.35 am on Tuesday 12 July 1949, and four-wheeled UEC open-balcony car 339 has had the 68, Erdington route, wound on to the blind especially for the photographer - this route was a Sunday working and was abandoned in 1923. Behind is Brush totally enclosed bogie car 611. There is a family resemblance between the two trams, but perhaps it is surprising to realise that the larger of the cars is, in fact, only nine years newer. Car 339 was withdrawn and broken up in October 1949, while 611 was taken out of service at the abandonment of the Lozells route on 30 September 1950. *W. A. Camwell*

Above left The view from the Villa Road terminus towards Lozells shows an area of early Victorian terraces of a superior design, with small railing-protected front gardens. Car 330, soon to be transferred from Witton to Coventry Road to replace the 71 Class Radial cars, stands in the single line stub on Monday 4 April 1938 in full prewar lined livery. This was the day that the Chamberlain Government announced that all British citizens would be measured for gas masks, in view of the deteriorating international situation. *H. B. Priestley*

Above right The busy junction of Villa Road and Hamstead Road at Lozells marked the start of the Villa Cross shopping centre. This was known as 'the village' and, as if to emphasise that nature, Bywater's shop on the left was embellished with mock-Elizabethan half-timber decoration. Car 624 leaves the section of single track as it passes into a short passing loop.

The bus is 1233 (FOF 233), a 1939 Daimler COG5 with an MCCW

body, and was withdrawn on 30 April 1950, only five months before the tramcar. It is working the 29A route from Kingstanding to Hall Green and is about to turn into Hamstead Road after the traffic lights have changed. Just visible on the left, where the young cyclist is negotiating the cobbles, is some abandoned track; this was part of a double junction that enabled the 25 service to Lozells to traverse Hamstead Road, and which was closed on 7 August 1933. *F. Lloyd Jones*

Below The police sergeant ambles past the few browsing shoppers in Villa Road as car 562, unusually carrying advertisements for two different brands of salad cream, works its way through the single line section on the 63 route on its way from Fort Dunlop. Beyond the distant 1947 Daimler CVG6 bus, 1580 (GOE 580), is the Villa Cross public house at the junction of Heathfield Road and Lozells Road. This Ansells pub had replaced an 18th-century inn during the 1920s and continued to serve this residential area until its closure in the mid-1980s. *R. T. Wilson*

Identical Brush trams 615 and 618, from the 587-636 Class, pass in the last section of double track in Lozells Road before reaching Six Ways, Aston. The shops and nearby houses were built in the 1870s, and this was a much better residential area than the nearby Summer Lane and Alma Street back-to-back developments that had been built twenty years earlier. In the distance, glimpsed between the trams, is the rather ornate Gothic-styled Christ Church of 1866. This stood on the corner of Victoria Road, up which car 618 will shortly go, and Witton Road, where the abandoned 3 route went. *F. Lloyd Jones*

Beyond Six Ways lay Victoria Road, and on a dim afternoon in late 1949 car 705 attracts the attention of a little girl as it clatters past. It was a notoriously noisy tram, having retained its spur gearing, while its 16 tons are no doubt taking their toll on what looks like fairly poor-quality track. In February 1926, when only a few months old, this car had been experimentally fitted with a pair of GEC 70 hp motors; the contrast with their normal GEC WT 32H 40 hp motors must have been impressive. As a result, Brush cars 512-536 were re-equipped with what proved to be the highest horse-power motors fitted to trams in Birmingham.

Car 705 has just left Six Ways, Aston, and is passing Wilton Street. Abbott's furniture store dominates one side of the junction, and its advertisements seem to be promoting the company and its merits rather than the furniture. This is not really surprising as much of the furniture sold at that time was of a limited range due to the early postwar restrictions. *R. T. Wilson*

Victoria Road crossed the 3X route at its junction with Park Road, then went down a steady gradient to meet the Lichfield Road tram routes. Here car 342 works the 5 route in 1950 and is travelling up the hill in Victoria Road. It has reached the curve which allowed depot access to Witton via Park Road and Witton Lane.

Car 342 was originally a standard member of the 100-strong 301 Class, with open balconies on a four-wheel truck. With the general improvement of tramway design welcomed by the public, BCT saw the value of enclosing the balconies on their trams. Unfortunately, the Board of Trade frowned upon double-deck narrow-gauge four-wheel tramcars being totally enclosed and only gave 'temporary' permission for 342 and the more successful 347 to be rebuilt. None the less, they both ran until 1950 as totally enclosed four-wheelers. Car 342 was not considered an aesthetic success and was known as the 'Armoured Car' for obvious reasons. *R. T. Wilson*

The 19th-century terraces of Lichfield Road at the Victoria Road junction were swept away in the early 1970s as part of a road improvement scheme. Strengthened car 562 turns into Victoria Road *en route* to Witton depot in the early evening of Thursday 2 July 1953. It has been overtaken by one of Sutton Coldfield garage's BMMO D5s, 3540 (MHA 540), whose body, like that of the tram, had been built by Brush Engineering. Car 562 was one of the cars fitted with 63 hp motors for faster running in the Handsworth area in the late 1920s, and was one of the cars whose body required considerable rebuilding in about 1948. This included the plating over of the lower saloon bulkhead windows with quarter-inch thick steel and the loss of the front ventilator on each side of the lower saloon. *T. J. Edgington*

After joining Lichfield Road, the 5 service followed the Erdington group routes to Salford Bridge. Few places in Birmingham can have changed as much as this once important junction. Today the concrete pillars of the elevated M6 Gravelly Hill interchange, known colloquially as 'Spaghetti Junction', have completely altered this scene. Car 613, a 1920 Brush bogie car, stands at the tram station shelters on 10 September 1950. This car was withdrawn prematurely in December 1952 after sustaining accident damage.

The shops behind reveal much about life at this time. J. H. Barker, the butcher, is advertising bacon and meat through the rationing scheme which was still in force. Next door, Broads Travel Bureau is promoting trips in the British Isles including holidays to Butlin's Holiday Villages and excursions to the Blackpool Illuminations. In the shop behind the tram shelter television sets are being enthusiastically advertised, although the standard-sized 9-inch black and white models were still something of a novelty. *A. N. H. Glover*

In order to return from Gravelly Hill to Lozells, the 5 route turned on to the reserved track in Tyburn Road. Here it used the first crossover to reverse to the Gravelly Hill tram shelters opposite the row of shops seen in the previous photograph.

Originally known as Salford Bridge Road and renamed on 25 November 1920, Tyburn Road was built with reserved track. It was a joint venture between the Transport Department and the Dunlop Tyre Company, who contributed to the road construction costs. Just visible behind the advertising hoardings on the left is the sandstone hill that had to be cut through in order that Tyburn Road could be linked to Gravelly Hill.

Car 720 stands after having its pole turned prior to moving over the crossover on 29 July 1939. This car would later be badly damaged when Witton depot was hit by a bomb on the night of Wednesday 4 December 1940. It was never repaired and was broken up at Moseley Road depot in May 1946. *H. B. Priestley*

This later view, of car 617, taken in Tyburn Road in 1950 is dominated by one of the cooling towers at Nechells power station. Car 617, along with others in the fleet, had undergone numerous changes from when it was built in 1920 by Brush. Although Birmingham's tramway design apparently stagnated after about 1924, a lot of developments to improve passenger comfort, speed of movement and reliability were implemented. Built with two 37 hp motors, by 1929 this car had been equipped with much faster DK30/1L 63 hp examples. The original open balconies had been enclosed by 1931, and upholstered, transverse seating had replaced the original longitudinal seats around 1928. In the late 1930s further improvements to the seating quality took place. Although never 'rehabilitated' in the same way that Chiswick Works did with London's trams, these traditional-looking blue and cream trams were thus steadily improved upon over the years. *L. W. Perkins*

ASTON ROAD ROUTES

The first electric tram route in Birmingham owned and operated by the Corporation formed the basis of the three main routes along Aston Road. These were the services to Erdington (2), Short Heath (78), and Pype Hayes (79).

The first route opened on Monday 4 January 1904 from Steelhouse Lane, initially to the Aston Corporation boundary at Aston Brook Street, but extended about a quarter of a mile across the Aston UDC boundary to Aston Cross on 16 June 1904. The cars which inaugurated this service were the 1-20 Class. These were large open-top 56-seater Brill 22E bogie cars built by the Electric Railway & Tramway Carriage Works Ltd (ER&TCW). By March 1905 the first ten had been top-covered and the remainder were completed in July 1907; this precluded them from passing beneath Aston railway bridge, and for most of the remainder of their careers they plied the nearby Perry Barr route.

A second service operated by the CBT depot at Witton ran from Aston Cross to Gravelly Hill along Lichfield Road and used single-deck cars and even some converted 'toast-rack' cable cars in order to get under Aston station bridge. After the bridge was raised, CBT used its standard

'Aston'-type four-wheelers, some of which were subsequently taken over by BCT in 1911.

On 22 April 1907, after much discussion of through running over Aston tracks, Birmingham trams, in the form of the small open-topped 21 Class cars, reached Erdington. This later became the 2 route and was the main service along the Aston and Lichfield Roads.

The stub terminus in Steelhouse Lane was near to both the main shopping thoroughfare of Bull Street and the Great Western Railway's Snow Hill Station in Colmore Row. The trams descended Steelhouse Lane, passing between the Law Courts and main city police station on one side and the General Hospital on the other. They then crossed the wide expanse of Corporation Place, crossing the Perry Barr route before travelling through an area of Victorian shops and three-storied terraced housing in Aston Street, Gosta Green and Aston Road.

From the Dartmouth Street junction to Aston Cross, the main road traversed a long row of small family-type shops and factories. Between the Birmingham & Fazeley canal and the eastern side of Aston Road North lay an area of small workshops and factories which continued to

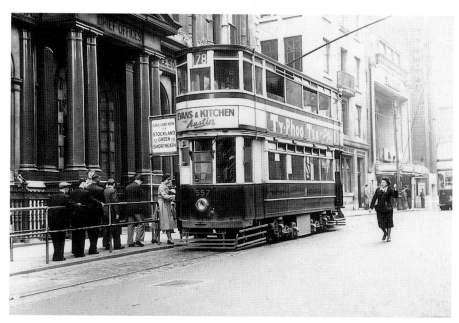

The conductress swings the trolley-pole round in order to allow car 557 to begin its return journey to Short Heath. The tram is standing outside the Wesleyan & General Insurance offices at the Steelhouse Lane terminus of the 78 route on Sunday 28 June 1953. This strengthened Brush-built tram of 1913 vintage is mounted on the standard Brush Burnley-type bogies. The leading driving wheels took up to 80 per cent of the total weight of the car, which gave excellent traction especially when accelerating and braking. The tram carries advertisements for Typhoo Tea, which was produced in Birmingham, and for Evans & Kitchen, one of the major Austin car dealers in the city. Car 557 saw service on the final day of BCT tram operation and was among the last trams broken up at Kyotts Lake Road Works in early August 1953. *T. J. Edgington*

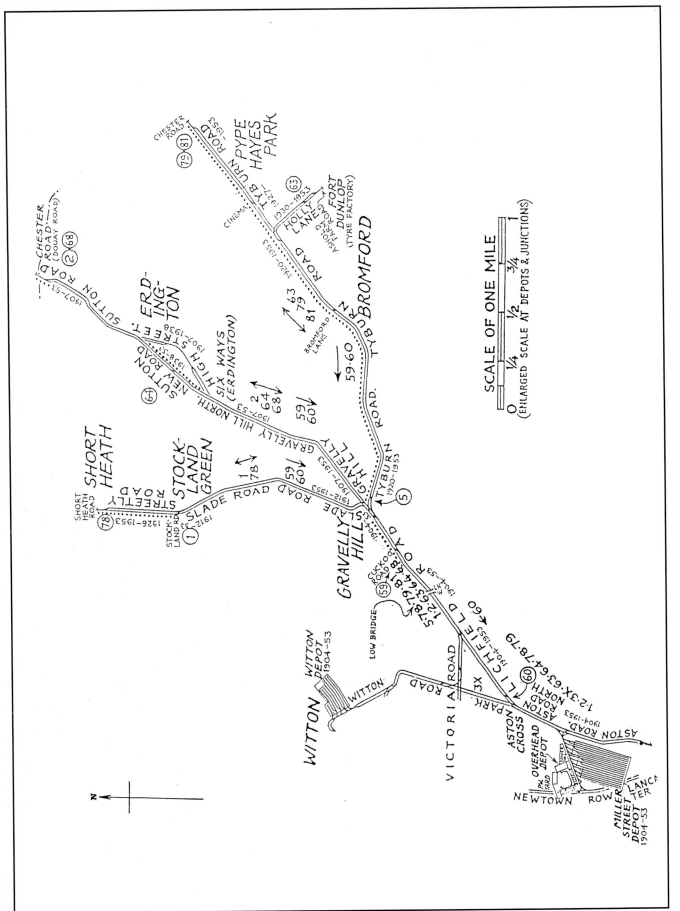

Aston Road routes

BIRMINGHAM TRAMS 1933-53

Aston Cross. This five-way junction saw the 3X tram and the Villa Park football specials continue in a northerly direction towards Aston Hall and the Witton terminus just beyond the depot, while the main route swung in front of the Ansells brewery, leaving behind the smells of brewer's malt mixed with the vinegar from Garton's HP Sauce factory.

Lichfield Road began to descend towards Aston station after the Lozells tram service came in on the western side from Victoria Road. The route then went through an area of yet more Victorian terraced housing until it reached Aston station bridge.

Beyond the bridge was an industrial area as far as the open expanse of Salford Park. Opposite was Cuckoo Road, which led by way of a humped-back bridge to the terminus of the first electric tram route to be abandoned, the Nechells service.

The area from Aston Bridge station was a mixed residential and industrial area and really marked the limit of pre-1914 urban expansion. The junction at Salford Bridge at the bottom of Gravelly Hill was the point where the three main Aston Road routes split. The 2 route carried on up Gravelly Hill through an area of superior Edwardian housing towards Six Ways, Erdington, while the Slade Road and Short Heath route turned left towards Stockland Green, and the Pype Hayes services turned right into the reserved track in Tyburn Road.

All three routes were operated mainly by all-electric bogie cars after the mid-1920s with the MRCW 637 Class and the Brush-built 662 Class being allocated for nearly all their working lives until the final abandonment on Saturday 4 July 1953.

Aston Road routes

The three main services along Lichfield Road shared a common city terminus in Steelhouse Lane. In this 1938 view a Standard saloon turns from Bull Street into Colmore Row while in the distance a 637 Class tram, resplendent in its lined-out prewar livery, stands at the terminus outside the Gaumont Cinema on the 2 route; the inspector and conductor, who are standing in front of their tram, have conspired to hide its identity. This part of the city has now completely disappeared, with a pedestrian underpass and a new Wesleyan Insurance building dominating the scene today. *D. R. Harvey collection*

Above Birmingham's last tramcar was car 616, which stands at the Steelhouse Lane terminus outside the Wesleyan & General Building on Saturday 4 July 1953. This view, taken from roof level, shows that despite the untidy end to the system, the population of Birmingham wanted to give the trams a worthy send-off. Car 616 left the city centre at 11.00 am, daubed with 'Birmingham's Last Tram' along the waist panels and 'The End' on both dashes. It was a sad and rather inauspicious end to 49 years of tramcar operation in the city, and it was a great pity that a more formal official ceremony could not have taken place. Car 616, carrying the Lord Mayor's party, followed similar car 623 to Erdington before returning to Miller Street for the last time. *L. W. Perkins collection*

Below In 1950, two bogie cars, Brush-bodied car 683 of 1924 on the 79 route and 573, a UEC-bodied tram on the 2 route, are about to pass over the crossover outside the Gaumont Cinema in Steelhouse Lane, whose canopy can be seen on the left. Today, all this is just a memory; the trams have obviously gone, but so has everything else. This part of Steelhouse Lane is the site of a gyratory traffic system outside the Birmingham Post & Mail Building in Colmore Circus. In this more leisurely scene, one can only wonder if the woman on the extreme right ever did pluck up enough courage to have her hair tinted. *A. B. Cross*

The delights of the Queen's Head public house do not seem to be able to entice any of the people in Steelhouse Lane as MRCW-bodied car 646 climbs the hill from the General Hospital towards the distant Gaumont Cinema and the Wesleyan & General Building in early 1953. The tram is carrying one of the most common of advertisements to appear in later years on Birmingham trams: the '3-In-One' oil advertisement was used extensively on the balcony panels of bogie cars from June 1951. Yet again, the small amount of vehicular traffic is noticeable, but more modern cars are beginning to appear on the scene, such as the Vauxhall Wyvern in the middle of the road, while beyond the tram is parked a Morris Oxford and a Jaguar Mark VII. *C. C. Thornburn*

Two cars, 700 and 694, neither carrying advertisements, travel up Steelhouse Lane from Corporation Place, passing the General Hospital. Built in 1897 using terracotta brickwork, the hospital was designed by the Victorian architect William Henman, who also built the Midland Hotel in the city centre. Opposite Whittall Street, soon to become the inward unloading terminus for the tram-replacement bus services for the Aston Road routes, is the rear of the Steelhouse Lane police station and the Victoria Law Courts. Its frontage on Corporation Street is a wonderful piece of late-19th-century civic pride, combining Gothic and Renaissance styles with terracotta brickwork. *F. Lloyd Jones*

At exactly 5.30 pm on 6 June 1953, just one month before the final abandonment, car 541, on the left, leaves the city on the 79 route, while car 696 is coming into the city from Short Heath. The trams are passing through the traffic island in Central Place; the Aston Road routes went straight on in the direction from which the rebuilt Midland Red Daimler CWA6 is coming. The replacing bus services would use Corporation Street to the left by the Central Fire Station's main entrance; this imposing building was opened by HRH the Duke of Kent on 2 December 1935, and replaced a large area of early Victorian shops and housing.

Just visible on the Fire Station is the bunting from the Coronation celebrations that had taken place just four days earlier. On that Saturday there had been a Coronation procession, involving some 7,000 troops, and this had caused the temporary closure of most of the city centre roads. *L. W. Perkins*

Looking in the opposite direction, we see two MRCW trams, cars 651 and 657, travelling down a nearly deserted Aston Street towards Central Place, with the Central Fire Station to their right. These cars, despite all the problems incurred with their delivery dates in 1923, put

in excellent service, covering a maximum mileage of 941,000 in 30 years. Their 40 hp motors did not exactly give sparkling performance, but, as they operated their entire lives from Miller Street depots, the extra power required on the hillier routes, such as Bristol Road, was not necessary. The distant building with the clock was Hawkins drapers shop, the only building which can be identified today; all the other buildings on the left were swept away in the development of the Aston University Campus in the 1970s. *C. C. Thornburn*

BIRMINGHAM TRAMS 1933-53

Carrying the advertisement for St Martin Chunky marmalade is 40 hp Brush-bodied car 687 of 1924. The elderly couple are in no rush to leave the tram as here, in Gosta Green, there is no other traffic. The tram will travel along Aston Road, passing, on the right, the Ionic-capitalled facade of the former Delicia Cinema. This old picture house still remains as a reminder of the more bizarre architectural styles associated with the early years of the cinema. It has variously been a BBC television studio and an Arts Theatre for Aston University. Another reminder of the types of building that have been demolished is the distant terrace of three-storied 19th-century houses; these would be cleared in the 1960s. To the right of the Austin pick-up van is where the 7 tram route, the first to be abandoned in Birmingham, formerly went on its way, via Lister Street, to Nechells. *C. C. Thornburn*

The junction of Aston Road and Dartmouth Street is today part of Dartmouth Circus, but on this sunny day, Monday 29 June 1953, it is still just another cobbled junction. Car 620 appears to be empty and is probably running into the city from Miller Street to undertake the duty to Barnabas Road, a shortworking of the 2 route that stopped halfway along Sutton New Road about a mile short of the actual terminus. The Austin KB8 Three-Way van is passing the Premier Garage, which is an agency for Austin cars; yet the only two new vehicles visible in their showrooms appear to be a Standard Vanguard Estate and a Land Rover! *T. J. Edgington*

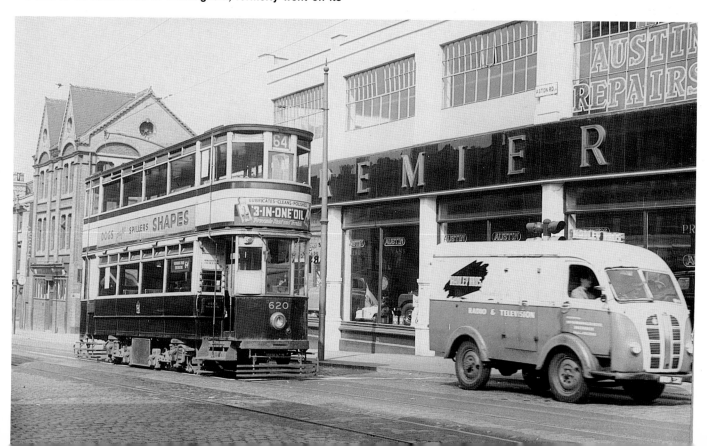

Above This fine view of strengthened MRCW car 623 belies the fact that this is the last day and that the tram is leading car 616 out of Miller Street to enact the closing ceremony on Saturday 4 July 1953. This car, like 616, had only been used occasionally in the previous 12 months, being stored in Kyotts Lake Road Works as a spare. The car had not been adulterated with the well-meaning but clumsily-produced 'Last Tram' lettering and had been especially cleaned for the occasion. In view of its apparently good condition, it seems sad that rather than being saved for preservation, it was broken up at Witton depot only ten days later. The only complete Birmingham tramcar preserved is four-wheel car 395, but the lower saloon of ex-Radial car 107 has now been saved for restoration. *D. R. Harvey collection*

Below Two boys roller-skate into Aston Road past the run-down Victorian terraces as car 639 reverses into Miller Street on 2 July 1953. This MRCW-bodied car was 40 years old and was typical of the BCT fleet operated from Miller Street in the last year of tramcar operation. Some 121 trams were extant at the start of 1953 and, although overhauling had ceased in 1951, cars still went through the works for mechanical attention. All the survivors were the older all-electric cars with 40 or 63 hp motors. These were chosen, rather than the later air-braked, high-horsepower trams because it was considered too expensive to retrain Miller Street depot drivers on the newer but unfamiliar tramcar types. *T. J. Edgington*

Built in 1911 as a standard BCT-style open-balconied UEC car, tram 347 was rebuilt in July 1921 with a totally enclosed top deck and served as the prototype for all the subsequent new cars in the fleet. Totally enclosed four-wheel double-deck cars on narrow gauge systems were considered by the Board of Trade to be unstable on exposed lines because of the extra upper saloon weight, but the four-wheel shortcomings of 347 were conveniently forgotten and it continued in service until September 1950. It stands opposite the entrance to Miller Street depot on 10 July 1949 on one of the ten sets of points which fanned into the depot. *A. N. H. Glover*

Cars 672, 679, 578 and 571 stand at the entrance to Miller Street depot. Time is running out for the trams as a replacement bus, a Crossley-bodied Daimler CVG6, stands among them. The Birmingham fleet of trams was not allowed to become run-down even in the last days of operation, but there is a certain dismal lack of sparkle to these elderly, dignified cars as they await another day's work. Unfortunately car 571, which is attracting some attention at the far end of the row, has a broken axle and will not run on the final two days of operation. *R. F. Mack*

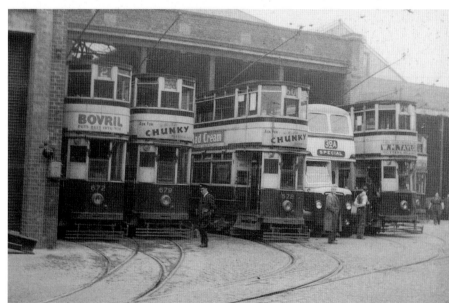

Opposite Miller Street depot was the Permanent Way Yard, which was used in the last few months of tramcar operation for overnight storage so that the conversion of Miller Street depot to bus operation could take place. Car 668, seen on the final Sunday before the closure, is carrying a CWS (Co-op) advertisement, one of the very few also to be carried by the contemporary bus fleet. It was a 40 hp Brush-built car of 1923 mounted on EMB Burnley maximum traction bogies. Like most of the 662-701 Class, eight of which were destroyed on the night of 9 April 1941, it operated the whole of its 28-year career from Miller Street.

Walking towards the photographer, with tripod in hand, is Norman Glover, whose photographs appear throughout this book. *T. J. Edgington*

Beyond Miller Street, the main road's name became Aston Road North. This busy street scene there shows that the shops near Aston Cross were small, family-owned retailers. Thompson's Fish Market seems to be attracting attention from the little boy, though the same scene today, with open fresh fish exposed to dust and traffic pollution, would be in contravention of practically every health and hygiene regulation.

The Ansell's lorry is fully laden with barrels of beer which are being delivered from the brewery just visible in the distance. It is being followed by a positively sparkling Austin K-type lorry. Amidst all this is car 729, working towards Aston Cross on the 78 route. The passengers are just alighting, seemingly with shopping bags at the ready, for another hunt for that elusive bargain. *D. Sanders collection*

Here again is car 668, passing along Aston Road North which was all but swept away in the early 1970s with the opening of the Aston Expressway. The tram route was lined with small factories and workshops; once the trams reached the distant Aston Cross, however, the industrial landscape became dominated by the HP Sauce factory and Ansell's brewery. This view of car 668 on the 78 route is taken from a following tram with, in the distance, another tram city-bound. Dominating the view is the 1882 bell tower of St Mary's church. *H. B. Priestley*

On the afternoon of 22 June 1953, at 3.39 pm, two trams, 583 on the 2 route and 665 on the 79, are seen at Aston Cross on their way into the city. Although this urban scene, looking down Lichfield Road, seems to have an air of permanence, this is deceptive. The clock was not the orginal one, and the Ansell's brewery had been built on the site of an old Georgian public house and was itself going to close in January 1981. The 30-year-old trams were already into their last two weeks of operation and would be replaced by Crossley, Daimler and Guy buses. Even the classic style of telephone box on the corner of Park Road is now all but phased out by British Telecom, as is the Belisha crossing, a 1930s device named after the then Minister of Transport, Leslie Hore-Belisha. *A. N. H. Glover*

The same view in July 1992 shows that only the library, the former Barclays Bank premises and the three-gabled shop remain at Aston Cross. Even the Ansell's brewery building has gone, having been closed in 1981 and replaced by a car showroom. MCW 'Metrobus' Mk II 2501 (POG 501Y) is coming into the city on the 114 route from Sutton Coldfield, negotiating the roadworks barrier at the approach to a new traffic island at the junction with Rocky Lane. The clock has been moved away from the island, altering the whole area out of recognition. *D. R. Harvey*

BIRMINGHAM TRAMS 1933-53

Above Another view of Aston Cross, where the tram-loading barriers were used by all the Lichfield Road routes. This busy intersection had also been served by the 3X tram to Witton which was abandoned on the last day of 1949; that route had followed the line of the buildings behind the clock tower. Car 721 is just manoeuvring over the crossover and its trolley-pole is already on the out-of-city wire; this in turn is delaying car 542 on its way to Erdington. This busy scene was taken on the last evening of operation when the Victorian suburb was still thriving and before urban renewal began to cater for cars rather than people. *T. J. Edgington*

Below Birmingham's last tramcar, 616, is seen performing 'the last rites' on its final journey to Erdington, passing the Ansell's brewery building at about 11.10 am on Saturday 4 July 1953. The heavily laden tram is on its way from Aston Cross, which it has just left, and is going towards Victoria Road, which is just beyond the brand new MCCW-bodied Guy 'Arab' IV bus in the distance. Car 616 attracts some attention from the Ansell's workers and the pedestrians as the passing of this tram meant also the passing of an era. Note the pillion rider following the tram with wreath held aloft. *C. Carter*

Above During the final morning of operation the trams were gradually taken out of service as they made the return trip to the city from the outer suburbs. This took place in Lichfield Road near Victoria Road, and passengers were transferred to waiting buses. Car 620, one of the 63 hp Brush 62-seater cars of 1920, turns into Victoria Road from Lichfield Road with the legend 'Now 66 bus' chalked on its dash panel. This had been one of the last trams to work the 79 route from Pype Hayes Park and was about to make the one-way trip to Witton depot, about two miles away. A total of forty-four trams were broken up there in July 1953 and car 620 would be one of them. *A. N. H. Glover*

Below Quite a traffic jam has developed behind car 647 as it negotiates the junction of Lichfield Road and Victoria Road in June 1953. Like the products advertised on the buildings on the left for Blue Mountain Rum and Mitchells and Butlers Nourishing Stout, the Victorian terraces of Lichfield Road have long since disappeared. They were built on cramped in-fill sites in a compact pattern of streets with houses opening on to the pavements like those to the right of the tram. Yet they were an improvement on the unhealthy and overcrowded back-to-back houses which had been built previously in Birmingham and Aston. *C. C. Thornburn*

The former LNWR railway bridge across Lichfield Road at Aston was rebuilt on Sunday 25 March 1906 to accommodate, initially, CBT's open-top electric double-deck cars. Although the road was subsequently lowered, it was always a tight squeeze to get a standard 15 ft 6 in top-covered tram beneath the bridge. The 1-20 Class, the 71-220 Class and most of the ex-CBT top-covered cars were officially barred from this route because of the bridge. Strengthened Brush car 556 is about to pass beneath it on its way to Short Heath on the last morning of operation. To provide sufficient clearance, the overhead wires were at the side of the road so that the trams' trolley-poles were level with the car roof. The tram is being followed out of the city by an Austin Big 7 of 1939 vintage, while an Austin K4 lorry approaches the bridge passing Holborn Hill on the extreme right, which led to Aston locomotive shed. *A. N. H. Glover*

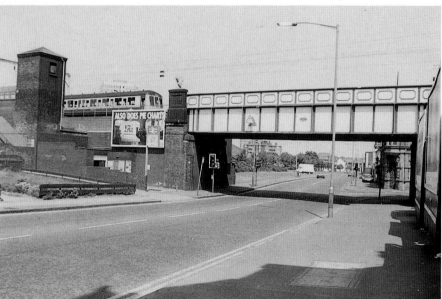

Lichfield Road, July 1992: all that remains is the railway bridge itself and the Swan and Mitre public house beyond, built in 1898 on the corner of Holborn Hill (in tram days it was the Swan Pool). All the old terraced shops and housing have been replaced by new low-rise developments and grassy open spaces. It is aesthetically more pleasing, but seems, somehow, to have lost the life and soul of the area. Only the barking exhaust of the diesel multiple unit as it leaves Aston station enlivens the scene. *D. R. Harvey*

Seen from beneath the bridge, car 693, working into the city, loads up with passengers at Holborn Hill early in May 1953, showing perfectly the disadvantages of trams stopping in the middle of the road and endangering the safety of the intending passengers. One wonders if, 40 years on, the lessons of their fathers and grandfathers haven't been passed on to some present-day bus drivers! On the advertising hoarding the popularity of Polo mints is high, but Al Read, who was top of the bill at the Birmingham Hippodrome that week, would only remain popular for another ten years or so, with his idiosyncratic Lancashire humour and catch phrases such as 'Right monkey' and 'I say, you'll be lucky!' *C. C. Thornburn*

Once beyond Aston Hall Road, Lichfield Road passed Salford Park and the junction with Cuckoo Road, where the tramway occupied a short 600-yard length of reserved track. Here 625, one of the Brush-bodied 63 hp cars, is working into the city on the 78 route from Short Heath. Although it is 1948, this car is still carrying the dignified, if somewhat shabby, fully lined-out prewar livery. Tram 625 was one of 354 bogie cars in Birmingham, all of which had maximum traction bogies; 625 was built with Brush Burnley units whose outer 31¹/₂-inch driving wheels can be identified by the higher positioning of the axle-boxes. *F. Lloyd Jones*

Car 661, numerically the last of the MRCW cars of 1923, is working the 2 route from Erdington on 7 June 1953. It has just crossed Salford Bridge, opened in 1926 to carry Lichfield Road over the River Tame and the Birmingham & Fazeley Canal. The tram is just about to enter the short section of reserved track in Lichfield Road which is protected by a pair of rather ornate bollards, one of which is visible in the foreground. The elderly flat-capped gentleman has time to sit on the bench on the left and watch the comings and goings at what was in 1953 a fairly busy stretch of road. Today he would soon be choked by exhaust fumes from the elevated M6 motorway at Gravelly Hill interchange; even Lichfield Road is today dominated by an almost never-ending traffic jam beneath the concrete motorway stilts. *J. H. Meredith*

Erdington

AS MENTIONED earlier, the junction at Salford Bridge at the bottom of Gravelly Hill was the point where the three main Aston Road routes split. The 2 route to Erdington, originally lettered 'E' until 1915, continued straight ahead and carried on through the busy and prosperous shopping centre of High Street, Erdington.

Increasing congestion led to the building of the Sutton New Road bypass in September 1938 and the trams were diverted on to this new reserved track route; this was the last section of new track opened in Birmingham. The last five-eighths of a mile of the route climbed Sutton Road, crossing Chester Road by passing through the middle of another traffic island, and reached the terminus latterly on a small piece of side reservation in the Edwardian shopping centre at the city boundary with Sutton Coldfield.

Brush car 692, working the 2 route from Erdington towards the city, is seen at Gravelly Hill on 22 June 1953 with its canvas sun-visor extended and carrying the typical St Martin Chunky marmalade and 'Say C.W.S. and Save' advertisements. The wires to the right are the 79 route along Tyburn Road to Fort Dunlop and Pype Hayes; the Short Heath 78 route turned to the left of the tram shelters and into Slade Road. Car 692 is beginning to show signs of platform sag, something which even a few years earlier would have been unknown. *A. N. H. Glover*

Inbound car 647 negotiates the Gravelly Hill junction as it passes a somewhat disinterested and underemployed police officer on traffic duty. On this wet Wednesday 15 September 1937 the tram has just descended Gravelly Hill and is about to stop at the tram shelters just beyond the junction. It has been surmised that BCT had planned that all the Erdington routes were to close as the penultimate set of routes in 1943; however, they were reprieved because of the ever worsening state of public transport during the Second World War. As it transpired it was the newer, more complicated air-brake cars running along the Bristol Road routes that were withdrawn in July 1952, a year before those to Erdington. *H. B. Priestley*

BIRMINGHAM TRAMS 1933-53

After the wide open spaces of Salford Bridge, the 2 route climbed up Gravelly Hill and on to the flatter but narrower road that led to the Six Ways, Erdington, junction. In this area the whole character of the route changed, becoming lined with large late-19th-century villas in their own grounds. This was something of a contrast with the houses just two miles further in towards the city. Car 653, one of the ubiquitous MRCW cars allocated to Miller Street depot, is working the 2 route and is just letting off a passenger at the Hunton Hill stop. The overtaking Austin Three-Way van of Marsh & Baxter takes up much of the remainder of the carriage-way. *C. C. Thornburn*

Birmingham's first traffic roundabout was put in at the complicated junction at Six Ways, Erdington, in 1926. The Birmingham custom of allowing tramcars to go through the centre of an island did little to improve traffic flow, while actually having a tram stop in the middle of the island appears, by today's standards, to be at best bizarre and at worst danger-ous! Brush-built car 608, one of nine of the class which was strengthened in 1948, leaves the tram stop on its way back to the city on the 2 route. On this sunny day in late June 1953 the majority of the windows are open, while the driver has obeyed the regulations and kept the lower saloon door shut. In the back-ground Crossley DD42/7 bus 2388 (JOJ 388) with a Crossley body negotiates the island, working the famous 25 miles long Outer Circle 11 route. *T. J. Edgington*

The trams originally travelled along High Street, Erdington, until September 1938. The fabric of this narrow road through the shopping centre has remained much the same since car 680 was working the 2 route through the suburb. The main difference is that Boots the Chemist was then a small shop; now, like many of its multi-national contemporaries, it is a large multi-produce store. Car 680 was one of the forty bogie tramcars ordered from Brush in 1924, and was one of eight of the 662 Class that was destroyed during the air raid which severely damaged Miller Street depot on 9 April 1941. *W. A. Camwell.*

Strengthened UEC car 558 of 1913 speeds along Sutton New Road beneath rather sagging overhead. This bypass route was introduced on 25 September 1938 and allowed for the 2 route and its shortworking, the 64 to Barnabas Road, to work along the central reservation. Only the Ford Anglia appears to have any desire for speed, as the elderly gentleman saunters across the almost deserted carriageway. It is 29 June 1953 and car 558 has only a week left in service. *T. J. Edgington*

In 1924 and 1925 Birmingham ordered 70 tramcars bodied by the Brush Company. Outwardly identical, the first forty cars of the 662 Class had Dick, Kerr DK30B 40 hp motors, while the 702-731 Class had GEC WT 32H 40 hp motors. Cars 691 and 726, one of each of the two types, pass on the central reservation of Sutton New Road at Barnabas Road in 1953. Cars such as 726 were considered sluggish compared with other classes working from Miller Street, but still amassed some 831,000 miles in the 28 years that they were in service. *C. C. Thornburn*

The July 1992 view of Sutton New Road shows the central reservation being used as a car park. The 62-seater trams have been replaced by 51-seater Leyland 'Lynx' LX2s. This particular bus, 1287 (G287 EOG), is being operated by Hockley garage and although not operating on an equivalent tramway route it does exemplify the changes that have taken place over the intervening years. All the major routes now use the bypass and only the buildings on the left beyond the other disappearing Leyland 'Lynx' can be readily identified from those in the previous view. *D. R. Harvey*

BIRMINGHAM TRAMS 1933-53

After leaving Sutton New Road, the narrow uphill climb of High Street was reached. Briefly capturing the feel of the hamlet that once was Erdington, the Georgian tiled-roof cottages bear testimony to years of neglect. Car 664, devoid of advertisements, is passing Erdington Roman Catholic church, built in the Decorated style in the mid-19th century. The entrance to the churchyard is at the lych-gate, which can be seen behind the trees. *F. Lloyd Jones*

The third traffic roundabout through which tramcars passed on the Erdington route was at the Sutton Road/Chester Road junction. Here, Car 677, one of the usual 40 hp Brush cars of the 662 Class, has just left the terminus and the driver is looking out for traffic on the island before accelerating across Chester Road. The Edwardian shopping area around the road junction was always considered to be a somewhat superior part of north Birmingham: 'a dormitory borough of considerable charm with a cross section of all social groups in the population, but an unusually large percentage of well-to-do business and professional people' (Municipal Review, 1955).

Sutton Road continued beyond the city boundary to Sutton Coldfield. Although Sutton had plans for a tram service, it never materialised. Midland Red took over the option on the route, although double-decker buses were not allowed into Sutton until the Second World War. This was because it was thought by the local residents that they might intrude into the privacy of large residential buildings along the route. *S. J. Eades*

The terminus of the Erdington service was on a short length of side reserved track in Sutton Road. Car 693 has to wait for the tram at the terminus to leave before it goes into the single-line stub beside the distant shelter, and judging by the distant figures of the driver and conductor of the other tram, the crew of car 693 have a considerable wait ahead of them. Few Birmingham bogie cars carried advertisements until after the Second World War, and when they did it tended to spoil their appearance. In this 1938 view, however, the fourteen-year-old Brush-bodied car has a number of dented panels and looks in need of a repaint. *D. R. Harvey collection*

Standing at the terminus on Sunday 7 June 1953, against the backcloth of early-20th-century shops, is car 581, waiting to return to Steelhouse Lane, some 5 miles away, while the crew pose for the photographer. The conductor is equipped with an 'Ultimate' ticket machine; this Miller Street-operated route was the first to be completely converted to this type of fare collection in 1949, and it took until 1954 to convert the whole system from the Bell Punch system. *A. N. H. Glover*

Slade Road and Short Heath

AS WITH all the Aston Road group of routes, Slade Road was worked from Miller Street depot. The original route was opened to Stockland Green and, when numbered in 1915, it was given the route number 1.

The route left the junction at Gravelly Hill and passed beneath the narrow former LNWR railway line to Sutton Coldfield and Lichfield. The section from the bridge to Stockland Green has perhaps changed least of all the Birmingham routes since abandonment, and still retains the feel of a prosperous, if somewhat older, residential area. The shops at Stockland Green marked the end of the route as first opened on 12 June 1912.

On 23 June 1926 the route was extended on reserved track into what was then virtually open country to serve the council estate that was under construction at Short Heath. Nearly 30 years after the abandonment the central reservation was rebuilt for the 'Trackline 65' experiments using the guided bus principle, which was in turn abandoned.

Unlike the civic ceremony which took place on 22 April 1907 when the Erdington route opened, the Stockland Green service along Slade Road appears to have opened quietly on Sunday 12 June 1912. On leaving Salford Bridge the route turned left into a short, narrow section of road where UEC bogie car 581 is seen on 29 June 1953. The original Stockland Green service, numbered 1, became a shortworking of the extended 78 service to Short Heath on 23 June 1926. *T. J. Edgington*

The former LNWR Aston and Lichfield railway line passed over Slade Road by means of an attractively porticoed skewed bridge, from which tramcar 542 has just emerged. It is the last morning of operation on the 78 route as this forty-year-old tram travels towards Salford Bridge and the city centre. Two trams could pass each other under the bridge but they took up virtually all of the road space; pedestrians were given the added protection of steel barriers under the bridge on one side of the road. The green Morris Commercial lorry of the Public Works Department on the left is parked on the wrong side of the road, although its workmen are nowhere to be seen. They would soon be involved in the ancillary work of the abandonment as they removed items of street furniture and the last vestiges of the tramway system. Perhaps they were installing the traffic lights to control the narrow entrance to the bridge when the replacement buses were introduced. *A. N. H. Glover*

Above Seen from the other side of the bridge in late June 1953, car 580 is working the 78 route on its way to the city. This bridge marked a real change in the urban landscape on the Short Heath route as Edwardian terrace houses with small gardens and bay windows took over from the basically industrial landscape towards Salford Bridge. On this sunny afternoon, the 40 hp UEC-built tram trundles along with only one more week to run in service. *T. J. Edgington*

Below Car 664 climbs up Slade Road past the terraced housing which lined most of the route to the original terminus at Stockland Green. Some distance behind the houses to the right lay the former LNWR railway station at Gravelly Hill, opened on 2 June 1863 on the line to Sutton Coldfield. This line encouraged the usual rapid urban growth, but left the short-haul journeys in need of street transport, which is why the tram routes benefited the local community and the short-distance passenger. *F. Lloyd Jones*

The original terminus at Stockland Green was typical of pre-First World War examples in Birmingham, consisting of a late-19th/early-20th-century shopping area at an important road junction. However, the extension of the tram route to Short Heath reduced the original terminus to just another shopping centre on the route. On 1 July 1953, the last Wednesday before the final closure, car 608 prepares to return to Miller Street under the anonymous destination 'Depot Only'. *G. F. Douglas*

This view of Stockland Green, looking out of the city a few days earlier on 29 June 1953, reveals the opening up of the road beyond Marsh Hill. The large building in the background is the Plaza Cinema, opened on Boxing Day 1927. Surprisingly, two other large suburban cinemas, the Robin Hood at Hall Green and the Crown in Icknield Port Road, were also opened on the same day. Car 713, one of the GEC-motored, Brush-built trams, stands at the old terminus, seemingly unsure whether it is a 59 shortworking to Gravelly Hill or a 78 going to the city; it was, however, common practice to leave different shortworking destinations on the blinds so they did not have to be changed by the conductor. The Typhoo tea advertisement about it being 'One of the good things about life' had replaced the more contentious one claiming that tea aided digestion. One wonders if the crew of the tram had one of those white enamel pots, which were standard BCT platform staff issue? If so, was it filled with Typhoo tea, brewed up for them in The Snack Bar? Or were the 'Delicious Ices' too much of a temptation? *T. J. Edgington*

Since the abandonment of the trams, Stockland Green has seen surprisingly few changes. In July 1992 Leyland 'Lynx' LX2, 1295 (G295 EOG), seems more certain of its destination than the tram did 39 years before. The Snack Bar has gone and Harper's shop has been replaced by the Gas and Electricity showroom. Yet the dormer-windowed Edwardian buildings remain surprisingly unaltered, while, in the background, the Plaza Cinema still stands, though now, almost inevitably, used as a bingo hall. *D. R. Harvey*

The Streetly Road tram extension from Stockland Green was opened on 23 June 1926 to serve a large new council house development. Former open-balconied Brush car 636, which had been totally enclosed in November 1931 at Kyotts Lake Road Works, has just left the terminus of the 78 route on 7 June 1953. By this time the state of the track left something to be desired and the rapid acceleration of the cars down the hill caused a considerable amount of 'hunting', or 'tail-wagging', even with these bogie cars. The central reservation was typical of the later Birmingham tram route extensions, being tree-lined, fairly straight and designed for high-speed running. *J. H. Meredith*

History almost repeated itself in October 1984 when the 'Trackline 65' experimental guided busway was opened in Streetly Road, covering virtually the same ground as the 1926 tram extension. The trees, which were planted after the trams were withdrawn in 1953, were removed, much to the annoyance of local residents, and, after a gap of 31 years, passenger vehicles were using the central reservation again. Newly delivered, silver and black painted MCW 'Metrobus' Mk II GR133/1 8111 (A111 WVP) is just about to enter the guided bus trackway at Edgware Road on 12 October 1984, just three days after its opening. Especially equipped with horizontal guide wheels, it would be used in this form only until September 1987, as the experiment was abandoned in favour of financial investment in the Light Rapid Transit system being planned for parts of the West Midlands. *D. R. Harvey*

Car 645 stands at the substantial shelters at the Short Heath terminus in the spring of 1953. It has evidently just arrived as its trolley-pole has not been turned for the return journey to the city centre. The driver's end of the tram is parked opposite the Bundy clock so that the driver could 'peg the clock' prior to leaving the terminus. The later reserved track extensions were well laid out and it was a pity that, once the last major extensions were built in the late 1920s, the lead that Birmingham Corporation had built up in tramway development was allowed to stagnate. *C. Carter*

94

Tyburn Road

AT GRAVELLY HILL the 79 route turned right into Tyburn Road which had been built with help from the Dunlop Tyre Company. Since the end of the First World War Dunlop had used a passenger barge to ferry its workers from the tram terminus at Salford Bridge along the Birmingham & Fazeley canal to the factory at Fort Dunlop. The route was opened on reserved track as far as Holly Lane on 13 May 1920 and extended to the gates of Fort Dunlop in Holly Lane on 13 February 1930. This was the last route extension in Birmingham and, unusually, was opened by ex-Radial car 172 which was fully decorated for the ceremony.

Originally the route along Tyburn Road was at the side of the road, but it became the central reservation some years later when the second, northern, carriageway was constructed. Tyburn Road was unusual in that it marked the boundary between residential and industrial landscapes. The latter occupied the River Rea side of the valley and the council housing the northern side.

Some way beyond Bromford Lane, where, after 1926, the Outer Circle bus service crossed the tram route, was the bus repair works. Just beyond was the Fort Dunlop turning into Holly Lane, and another hundred yards or so further was the junction with Kingsbury Road.

The route was extended by about three-quarters of a mile to Chester Road at Pype Hayes Park as the 79 route on 20 February 1927.

The reserved track along Tyburn Road was partly financed by Dunlop and, until the municipal housing development began, it ran through open country to the factory. Here car 580 demonstrates both the advantages and disadvantages of reserved track operation: the trams were certainly separated from the traffic - although in this 4 May 1953 view there is parlously little need for such separation - but the main difficulty was that passengers had to cross the road in order to reach the tram stop.

Behind the trees on the right is the large bus repair works opened in 1929 and closed early in 1933. It is one of the ironies of the BCT system that after 1937, when the Stratford Road routes closed, the bus repair works was on a tram route and the tram repair works was on a bus route! *C. C. Thornburn*

UEC-built tram 571 slowly reverses across the tracks near the original Tyburn Road terminus at Holly Lane on 30 June 1953. Tyburn Road is unusual in that the north-west side is 1920s municipal housing and the south-east side consists of factory units occupying the land on the terraces above the River Tame. The lowest land, nearest the river, was used largely in connection with the purification of sewage, although above the flood plain were numerous larger factory units such as Fort Dunlop and the Fisher & Ludlow car body factory. The factories which actually lined Tyburn Road, as can be seen behind the tram, were much smaller units often doing the sort of engineering that gave the city its famous industrial heritage. *T. J. Edgington*

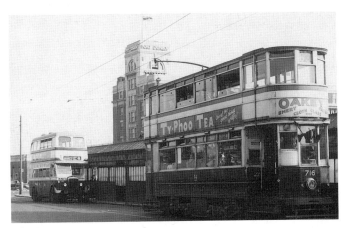

Left The Fort Dunlop siding was opened on 13 February 1930 when suitably decorated car 172 carried civic dignitaries back to the city centre. This was the penultimate tramway extension in Birmingham and was built into Holly Lane, which was a private road belonging to the Dunlop company. It was an impressive layout, with kerbside loading against a background of playing fields and factory reminiscent of the Cadbury factory at Bournville. Cars 693 and 717 are seen here at the siding on 22 June 1953. *A. N. H. Glover*

Above On a sunny afternoon, 20 June 1953, Brush-built 63-seater car 716, equipped with EMB Burnley bogies and the rather slow Dick, Kerr DK30/1L 40 hp motors, stands at the tram shelters in Holly Lane. The impressive Fort Dunlop proclaims the name of the Belfast veterinarian who invented the pneumatic tyre in 1888, although he was bought out by other entrepreneurs, such as E. T. Hooley, as early as 1895. By 1915 a 260-acre site had been chosen in open countryside in the Tame Valley and here Fort Dunlop was built, the somewhat military tower of which dominates the skyline. Behind the tram is 1950 MCCW-bodied Daimler CVD6 2029 (JOJ 29), the penultimate exposed-radiator Daimler bus supplied to BCT. These were probably the quietest and most refined of all Birmingham's postwar half-cab double-deckers. *T. J. Edgington*

About to leave the reserved track on Tyburn Road at Kingsbury Road is UEC car 579. As can be seen, the bulkhead platform window has been plated over, revealing this to be one of the strengthened 40 hp cars, rebuilt in this form in December 1948 with EMB bogies and DK30B motors. In retrospect, it seems a lot of capital expenditure for only 4½ years of further service. The maintenance on the reserved track, with the encroaching weeds, seems to be becoming a little neglected by this date, as does the tram itself. *C. C. Thornburn*

BIRMINGHAM TRAMS 1933-53

Right MRCW-bodied tram 644 of 1923 is seen shortly after leaving the terminus at Pype Hayes on the 79 route. The council housing was developed throughout the outer suburbs of the city in the interwar period, the Pype Hayes development containing 1,344 houses, but ranking it only 12th out of 15 major housing schemes built between the wars. Some of the houses can be seen on the right-hand side of this view of Tyburn Road taken in 1948.

Car 644 was involved in an accident in December 1952 and was sold to W. T. Bird of Stratford-upon-Avon. This company was given the task of breaking up all the trams after 1950 and was well known for its scrapyard which also contained many of Birmingham's former bus fleet. *F. Lloyd Jones*

Above The driver and conductor of Brush-bodied car 672 stand with their trusty tram at the Pype Hayes terminus on 17 May 1953. They look at both the car and the photographer with a slightly bemused expression, perhaps wondering why anyone would want to photograph their forty-one-year-old tram. The 79 route was opened on 20 February 1927 from Holly Lane to Pype Hayes to serve the small-windowed world of the council house estate. Behind the speeding Ford V8 Pilot is the Bagot Arms, typical of the huge public houses which were built at this period on these interwar housing estates. *A. N. H. Glover*

Despite all the contractual problems with their construction and delivery, the MRCW cars proved to be a very sound investment for BCT, and only six of the 637-661 Class failed to see service over the last few days of operation. Car 657 is seen here alongside the distinctive wooden shelters erected at the end of the reserved track routes, with the entrance to Pype Hayes Park beyond the trees on the other side of Chester Road. *G. Wood*

POSTSCRIPT: One of the last four-wheel cars to be scheduled for breaking up in November 1950 was UEC-bodied tram 395. However, the City Museum and Art Gallery requested that a Birmingham tramcar should be preserved, and as a result car 395 was taken off the scrapping list and used as a shunter at Kyotts Lake Road Works until it was prepared for renovation under the watchful eye of the Works Superintendent, P. W. Lawson. The tram was presented to the museum after its renovation, funded by the Birmingham Common Good Trust in June 1953.

It is seen here at the Rubery terminus of the 71 route in the mid-1930s. This terminus will feature in the next volume when the routes on the south and west sides of the city will be examined. *W. A. Camwell*

BIRMINGHAM CORPORATION TRAMCAR FLEET

1-20

Built 1903; into service 4.1.1904. ER&TCW open-top, four-bay bodies, reverse stairs, open platform. Seating capacity 28/28. Mounted on Brill 22E bogies. Dick, Kerr DK25 25 hp motors. Remotored DK6A 35 hp motors 1905. Open balcony top-covers fitted 1905 or 1907. Platforms vestibuled and normal stairs fitted 1924-9. Fitted with EMB Burnley bogies 1923-5, except 4, 9, 10 and 16 which had Brush Burnley bogies. Fitted with Dick, Kerr DK30B 40 hp motors 1923-5. Cars 1-2/4-7/10-12/14/16 destroyed in air raids 1940-41. Rest of class withdrawn 12.1949.

21-40 Built 1905
41-70 Built 1905-6
221-270 Built 1907
271-300 Built 1908

UEC open-top, three-bay bodies, open platforms. Seating capacity 26/22. Mounted on Brill 21E 6 ft 0 in trucks. Dick, Kerr DK25 25 hp motors. Top-covers fitted to all 1911-25, except 266 which was used as the Illuminated Car 1909-29. All except 28 cars vestibuled 1923-8. Cars 41-70/221-222/234/237-239/243-244/247-252/254-256/259-265 fitted with Maley track brake 1909-10. Most Brill-Maleys fitted with Dick, Kerr DK13A 40 hp motors 1919-22. Various cars fitted with Fischer bow-collectors from 1924. Car 28 cut down to single-deck for 1916 trailer experiments. Withdrawals 7.1930-3.1937; last withdrawals of Lodge Road Brill-Maleys with bow-collectors 3.47.

71-220

Built 1906-7. UEC top-covered, four-bay bodies with open balconies and platforms. Seating capacity 28/24. Mounted on Mountain & Gibson 8 ft 6 in radial trucks. All retrucked 1923-28; Dick, Kerr 6A 35 hp motors. Cars 82/101/146/152/163/213 with UEC Preston trucks. Cars 89/115/125/157-158/161/168/173/208 with Brush trucks. All remaining 135 cars fitted with Brush Peckham P35 pendulum trucks. All vestibuled 1923-30. From 1926 102 cars fitted with BTH GE249A 35 hp motors. Twenty-one cars fitted with DK13A 40 hp motors 1934-7. Withdrawals 1.1937-9.1939. Cars 73/87/89/97/99/104/109/111/113/116/125/137/142/144/160/170/172/176-7/183/207/210 retained for emergency use throughout Second World War.

301-360 Built 1911
361-400 Built 1911-12

UEC top-covered, four-bay bodies with open balconies. Seating capacity 28/24. Mounted on UEC 7 ft 6 in swing-yoke trucks. Dick, Kerr DK 13A 40 hp motors. Cars 361/367-8/375/379 converted to single-deck 1917-23. Car 342 (1.1921) and 347 (7.1921) fitted with totally enclosed vestibules. Car 341 cut down to single-deck for use as VE Day Illuminated Car; converted to supply car 1948-52. First withdrawal 1923. Cars 303/7/24/60/90 damaged in air raid in 1940. Rest of class withdrawn by 10.1950. Car 395 preserved in Birmingham Museum of Science and Industry.

401-450

Built 1912. UEC top-covered, four-bay bodies with open balconies. Seating capacity 30/24. Mounted on M&G 7 ft 6 in trucks. Dick, Kerr DKl9A 40 hp motors. Spencer, Dawson air and oil brake. Car 431 converted to single-deck 1916-23. Car 439 withdrawn 1941. Rest of class withdrawn 10.1949.

451-452 (ex-CBT 178/180)

Built 1903. CBT open-top, reverse staircase, five-bay bodies. Seating capacity 34/34. Mounted on Brush equal wheel bogies. Brush 1002B 25 hp motors. Fitted with BCT Burnley bogies and Dick, Kerr DKl9A 40 hp motors 1913-4. Remotored with Dick, Kerr DK 13A 40 hp motors 1924-6. Converted to vestibuled single deck 1917-22. Fitted with open balcony, top covers 1926. Withdrawn 12.1949.

453-468 (ex-CBT 193-208)

Built 1904. Brush open-top, unvestibuled, four-bay bodies. Seating capacity 26/22. Mounted on Brush 8 ft trucks. Brush 1002D 25 hp motors. Remotored with Dick, Kerr DK6A 35 hp motors 1919-24. Fitted with vestibuled top-covers with open balconies 1923-5. Withdrawn 1937-9.

469-472 (ex-CBT 239-242)

469 Built 1904 by Brush for Birmingham & Midland Tramways
470-472 Built 1904 by CBT

Open-top, unvestibuled, four-bay bodies. Seating capacity 26/22. Mounted on Brush 8 ft trucks. Brush 1002D 25 hp motors. Cars 470-472 remotored with Dick, Kerr DK6A 35 hp motors 1922-4. Fitted with vestibuled top-covers with open balconies 1923-8. Withdrawn 1925-38.

473-480 (ex-CBT 181-188)

Built 1903. Brush open-top, unvestibuled, four-bay bodies. Seating capacity 29/26. Brush D bogies. Fitted with Brush Lycett & Conaty 8 ft 6 in Radial trucks 1905. Brush 1002D 25 hp motors. Cars 474/5/8/80 fitted with Dick, Kerr DK6A 35 hp motors 1919-21. Fitted with vestibuled top-covers with open balconies 1925. Unmodified cars withdrawn 1924; rest of class withdrawn 1938.

481-483 (ex-CBT 212-214)

Built 1904. CBT open-top, unvestibuled, four-bay bodies. Seating capacity 26/22. Brush Lycett & Conaty 8 ft 6 in trucks. Brush 1002D 25 hp motors. Fitted with Dick, Kerr DK6A 35 hp motors 1921-4. Fitted with vestibuled top-covers with open balconies 1923-4. Withdrawn 1938-9.

484-501 (ex-CBT 220/222-227/229/231/233-234/236-238/246-247 249/251)

Built 1904-5. Brush open-top, unvestibuled, four-bay bodies. Seating capacity 26/22. Brush Lycett & Conaty 8 ft 6 in trucks. Brush 1002B 33 hp motors. All class, except cars 493/8, fitted with Dick, Kerr DK6A 35 hp motors 1913-24. Cars 484/89/91 fitted with Brill 121E 6 ft trucks 1920-1. Withdrawn 1937-9.

502-511 (ex-CBT 152/154/156/158/160/162/164/166/168/170)

502-508 Built 1901 by ER&TCW
509-510 Built 1901 by CBT
511 Built 1903 by CBT

Open-top, reverse staircase, unvestibuled, four-bay bodies. Seating capacity 26/22. Mounted on Peckham 6 ft 9A cantilever trucks. BTH GE58 35 hp motors. Fitted with Brill 21E trucks 1913. Class withdrawn 1913-28. Most converted to Permanent Way cars.

512-586

Built 1913-4. UEC four-bay bodies with open balconies. Seating capacity 34/28. Mounted on M&G Burnley bogies. Dick, Kerr DK19A 40 hp motors. Vestibuled 1926-30. Cars 512-562/5-6 fitted with BTH GE249A 37 hp motors 1918-22. Car 563 fitted with DK30B 40 hp motors 1920. Cars 564/67-86 fitted with Dick, Kerr DK13A 40 hp motors 1920-3. Cars 537-562/5-6 fitted with Dick, Kerr DK30/1L 63 hp motors 1925-7. Cars 512-536 fitted with GEC WT 32R 70 hp motors 1927-8. EMB Burnley bogies and Dick, Kerr DK30B 40 hp motors fitted to cars 551/69-73/6-81/3-6 1943-51. Cars 564/67-8/74-5/82 destroyed in air raids 1941. Cars 525/538 withdrawn in Second World War; rest of class withdrawn 1950-3.

587-636

Built 1920-1. Brush four-bay bodies with open balconies. Seating capacity 34/28. Mounted on Brush Burnley bogies. BTH GE 249A 37 hp motors. Vestibuled 1927-31. Car 630 equipped with EMB Maley air-brakes 1923. Withdrawn 1949-53.

637-661

Built 1923-4. MRCW totally enclosed bodies. Seating capacity 35/28. Mounted on EMB Burnley bogies. Dick, Kerr 30B 40 hp motors. Withdrawn 1952-3.

662-681 Built 1924
682-701 Built 1924-5

Brush totally enclosed bodies. Seating capacity 35/28. Mounted on EMB Burnley bogies. Dick, Kerr DK30B 40 hp motors. Cars 663/9-70/80-1/5/97/99 destroyed in air raid 1941. Rest of class withdrawn 1952-3.

702-731

Built 1925. Brush totally enclosed bodies. Seating capacity 35/28. Mounted on EMB Burnley bogies. GEC WT32H 40 hp motors. Cars 702-3/7/8/11/4/8/20/3/4/7 withdrawn 1940-1. Rest of class withdrawn 1953.

732-761

Built 1926. Brush totally enclosed bodies. Seating capacity 35/28. Mounted on EMB Burnley bogies. Dick, Kerr DK30/1L 63 hp motors. EMB air wheel and track brakes. Withdrawn 1952.

762-811

Built 1928. Brush totally enclosed bodies. Seating capacity 35/27. Mounted on EMB Burnley bogies. Dick, Kerr DK30/1L 63 hp motors. EMB air wheel and track brakes. Fitted with bow collectors 1928-50. Car 785 destroyed in air raid 1941. Rest of class withdrawn 1952.

812-841

Built 1928-9. Short Bros totally enclosed bodies. Seating capacity 35/27. Mounted on M&T Burnley bogies. Dick, Kerr DK30IL 63 hp motors. M&T air wheel and track brakes. Car 821 withdrawn 1941. Rest of class withdrawn 7.1952.

842

Built 1929. Short Bros totally enclosed lightweight bodies. Seating capacity 36/27. Mounted on EE lightweight Burnley bogies. Dick, Kerr DK T105/3KP 40 hp motors. M&T air wheel and track brake. Re-equipped with M&T Burnley bogies ex-821 1950. Withdrawn 7.1952.

843

Built 1930. Brush totally enclosed lightweight bodies. Seating capacity 33/27. Mounted on M&T Burnley bogies. GEC WT28AS 40 hp motors. M&T air wheel and track brakes. Withdrawn 1.1952.

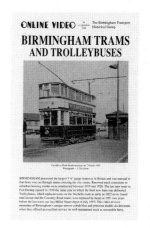